le clocher
L'AVION
le vignoble
COIFFEUR.
le poteau
le monument
la grille
cochon
l'auto
le curé
le mur
la fourche
le gendarme
la femme
le sac
la brouette
panier
le chasseur
la vache
la poupée
le lapin
le chien
le docteur
la veuve
Goetz

H. Millman

ESSENTIAL FRENCH VOCABULARY

By W. F. H. Whitmarsh, M.A., L. ès L.

A FIRST FRENCH BOOK

A SECOND FRENCH BOOK

A THIRD FRENCH BOOK

A FOURTH FRENCH BOOK

Selections from A SECOND and THIRD FRENCH BOOKS on a set of 2 L.P. Records

A FIRST FRENCH READER

A FRENCH WORD LIST

ESSENTIAL FRENCH VOCABULARY

SIMPLER FRENCH COURSE FOR FIRST EXAMINATIONS

COURS SUPÉRIEUR

LECTURES POUR LA JEUNESSE

MORE RAPID FRENCH, BOOKS 1, 2 and 3

MODERN CERTIFICATE FRENCH

SENIOR FRENCH COMPOSITION

By W. F. H. Whitmarsh, M.A., L. ès L., and C. D. Jukes, M.A.

ADVANCED FRENCH COURSE

NEW ADVANCED FRENCH COURSE

ESSENTIAL FRENCH VOCABULARY

REVISED EDITION

BY

W. F. H. WHITMARSH, M.A.

LICENCIÉ ÈS LETTRES

LONGMAN

LONGMAN GROUP LIMITED
London

Associated companies, branches and representatives throughout the world

First published 1956
Second edition 1972
Fourth impression 1976
Seventh impression 1980

ISBN 0 582 36087 0

The endpaper is reproduced from a drawing by Walter Goetz from the book, *Les Carnets du Major Thompson*, by Pierre Daninos, published by Librairie Hachette.

Printed in Singapore by
New Art Printing Co Pte Ltd.

FOREWORD

To assemble the material for this book, the author first established a basic vocabulary of high-frequency words, to which were added words which had occurred in G.S.C. and G.C.E. ("O" Level) examination papers over a number of years. Thus one can be sure that this Vocabulary contains practically all the words which pupils are likely to require in their preparation for the Ordinary Level test.

In Part I, rather more than 2,000 words have been marshalled in 90 groups, the classification being based very largely on the association of ideas. There are no rigid divisions into parts of speech, since verbs, nouns, adjectives and adverbs which derive from one another need to be kept in the same group. This arrangement may not be ideal, but then there is no ideal arrangement. How is it possible to classify a large amorphous vocabulary to suit all purposes? It is hoped, however, that the present classification will prove particularly useful for free composition and for oral work.

Part II provides a fairly extensive English to French vocabulary arranged in alphabetical order. This will be useful to the pupil when he is practising *thème* and when, in the course of writing a free composition, he needs to verify specific points of expression. As it is the policy of Examining Boards to restrict the vocabulary of the *thème* to reasonably common words, the present list should prove adequate for all *thèmes* done in the Examination year.

Apart from its use in schools, this list should prove useful to those who wish to refresh or enlarge their knowledge of French words and expressions.

W.F.H.W.

NOTE TO THE SECOND EDITION 1972

While the aim of this work was to assemble and set out the basic and enduring vocabulary of the French language, the Publishers felt that after a lapse of some years the work should be brought up to date by the inclusion of some words and phrases much used today and having a bearing on contemporary life. Accordingly the author has scrutinized his lists and has made a number of changes, eliminating some things of questionable value and inserting words or phrases of more modern interest.

W.F.H.W.

FOREWORD

To collect the material for this book the author first established a basic vocabulary of high frequency words, to which were added words which had occurred in G.C.E. and C.S.E. [illegible] French examination papers over a number of years. The student can be sure that this Vocabulary contains practically all the words which pupils are likely to require in their preparation for the Ordinary Level test.

In Part I, rather more than 2000 words have been classified in 40 groups, the classification being based very largely on the association of ideas. These are divided into parts of speech, since verbs, nouns, adjectives and adverbs which come from one root need to be kept in the same group. This arrangement may not be [illegible] ideal arrangement. [illegible] vocabulary [illegible] purposes. It is hoped, however, that the topical classification will prove particularly useful for free composition and for oral work.

Part II provides a fairly extensive English to French vocabulary arranged in alphabetical order. This will be useful for the pupil who [illegible] in the course of writing a free composition [illegible] point of expression. [illegible] vocabulary of the [illegible] should prove adequate for [illegible].

[illegible] in schools, the list should prove useful to those who wish to refresh or enlarge their knowledge of French words and expressions.

NOTE TO THE SECOND EDITION [illegible]

With [illegible] vocabulary of the French language, the Publishers felt that after a lapse of some years the work should be brought up to date by the inclusion of some words which have [illegible] and having [illegible] the author [illegible] has also made a number of [illegible] and [illegible] of [illegible] and [illegible] in their present [illegible].

CONTENTS

PART I

FRENCH WORDS CLASSIFIED

NOTE ON VERBS

Attendre (*vendre*) means that *attendre* is conjugated like ***vendre***, which figures in the Verb List at the end of the book. All verbs about which there may be any question are dealt with in this way. For instance **offrir** (*ouvrir*) indicates that one should consult *ouvrir* in the Verb List.

In the case of some verbs an example is provided showing the construction the verb takes. For instance, under **arracher**, *to snatch*, we provide the example "je lui arrachai le pistolet". This is to remind you that "to snatch something from somebody" is, in French, *arracher quelque chose à quelqu'un*. All the examples are intended to be helpful and should be carefully noted.

ABBREVIATIONS USED

adj., adjective
adv., adverb
conj., conjunction
fam., familiar
fut., future
invar., invariable
irr., irregular
p. hist., past historic
pl., plural
prep., preposition
subj., subjunctive
trans., transitive
intrans., intransitive

1. FAMILY AND FRIENDS

la famille, family.
les parents (*m.*), parents ; **le parent**, *f.* **la parente**, relation, relative.
le père, father.
le mari, husband
la mère, mother.
la femme, wife, woman.
la veuve, widow.
le fils, son.
la fille, daughter ; girl.
le frère, brother.
la sœur, sister.
l' oncle, uncle.
la tante, aunt.
le neveu, nephew.
la nièce, niece.
le cousin, *f.* **la cousine**, cousin.
le grand-père, grandfather.
la grand'mère, grandmother.
les grands-parents, grandparents.
le petit-fils, *pl.* **les petits-fils**, grandson.
la petite-fille, *pl.* **les petites-filles**, granddaughter.
le beau-père, father-in-law.
la belle-mère, mother-in-law.
le gendre, son-in-law.
la bru, daughter-in-law.

ressembler (à), to resemble, to be like, *e.g.* **tu ressembles à ton père.**
le nom, name ; **nommer**, to name ; **il se nomme Jean** *or* **il s'appelle Jean**, his name is John.

un ami, *f.* **une amie**, friend ; **l'amitié** (*f.*), friendship.
le (la) camarade, comrade, friend.
le compagnon, *f.* **la compagne**, companion.
le copain, *f.* **la copine** (*fam.*), pal, " mate ".
le voisin, *f.*, **la voisine**, neighbour ; **le voisinage**, neighbourhood.

2. PEOPLE IN GENERAL

un homme, man ; **le bonhomme**, (old) fellow.
le monsieur, *pl.* **les messieurs**, gentleman.
le célibataire, bachelor.
la vieille fille, spinster.
la femme, woman, wife.
la dame, lady.
un(e) enfant, child.
le gamin, *f.* **la gamine**, youngster ; " kid ".
le bébé, baby.
le garçon, boy, lad ; (*in café or restaurant*) waiter.
la fille, daughter, girl ; **la jeune fille**, girl (*over* 13 *or* 14) ; **la fillette**, girl (*up to* 13 *or* 14).

la demoiselle, young lady.
la personne, person.
un individu, individual.
un être humain, human being.
les gens, people ; **les jeunes gens**, young men (fellows).
le monde, world ; people ; **tout le monde**, everybody ; **beaucoup de monde**, a lot of people.
le peuple, people (*of a nation*) ; ordinary people.
la foule, crowd ; **en foule**, in a crowd, in crowds.
la société, society ; company, party (*of people*).
la bande, party, troop ; gang.
le cortège, procession.

seul, alone ; only ; **seulement**, only.
unique, sole, (one and) only, *e.g.* son fils unique ; **uniquement**, only, merely.
ensemble, together.
s'assembler *or* **se rassembler**, to assemble, to gather, *e.g.* une foule s'assembla.
réunir (finir), to bring together ; **se réunir**, to gather, to meet, *e.g.* ils se réunissent deux fois par an.
rejoindre (craindre), to join *or* rejoin, *e.g.* il rejoignit ses parents.
se séparer, to separate, to part, *e.g.* ils se séparèrent à minuit.

3. PERSONS : OTHER USEFUL WORDS

le roi, king ; **la reine**, queen ; **le règne**, reign ; **sous le règne de**, in the reign of ; **régner**, to reign.
le prince, prince ; **la princesse**, princess.
le seigneur, lord.
le valet, valet, footman.
un avocat, lawyer, barrister.
le confrère, colleague, associate.
le témoin, witness.

le géant, giant.
la fée, fairy ; **le conte de fées**, fairy-tale.
le polisson, scamp, little rascal.
le coquin, rogue.
le voleur, thief, robber ; **voler**, to steal (*also* to fly).
le lâche, coward ; **lâche** (*adj.*), cowardly.
le mendiant, beggar ; **mendier**, to beg.

4. LIFE IN GENERAL

la vie, life ; **en vie**, alive ; **risquer la vie**, to risk one's life ; **gagner sa vie**, to earn one's living.

vivre (*irr.*), to live ; **vivant**, living, alive ; **survivre (à)**, to survive, outlive, *e.g.* il survécut à son fils.

exister, to exist ; **l'existence** (*f.*), existence.

la **mort**, death.

mourir (*irr.*), to die ; **mort**, dead ; **il est mort**, he has died.

périr (finir), to perish.

le **sort**, lot.

le **destin**, fate.

la **naissance**, birth ; **naître** (*irr.*), to be born ; **il est né**, he was born ; **natal**, native, *e.g.* sa ville natale.

le **berceau**, cradle ; birthplace.

l' **enfance** (*f.*), childhood.

jeune, young ; **la jeunesse**, youth.

vieux, *f.* **vieille**, old ; **le vieillard**, old man ; **la vieillesse**, old age ; **vieillir** (finir), to age, to grow old.

le **mariage**, marriage ; **se marier**, to be married ; **épouser**, to marry, *e.g.* il épousa une Américaine ; la **mariée**, bride ; **le marié**, bridegroom.

la **noce**, wedding.

l' **âge** (*m.*), age ; **quel âge avez-vous?** how old are you? **j'ai seize ans**, I am sixteen ; **il est âgé de vingt ans**, he is twenty.

aîné(e), elder ; **l'aîné(e)**, eldest.

l' **anniversaire** (*m.*), birthday.

5. SOCIAL RELATIONSHIPS

connaître (*irr.*), to know ; **la connaissance**, acquaintance ; **reconnaître**, to recognize ; **la reconnaissance**, recognition ; gratitude ; **inconnu**, unknown.

aimer, to like, to love ; **aimable**, nice, pleasant ;

l' **amour** (*m.*), love.

adorer, to adore.

admirer, to admire ; **admirable**, admirable, lovely.

flatter, to flatter.

le **compliment**, compliment.

le **plaisir**, pleasure ; **avec plaisir**, with pleasure.

le **cadeau**, present, gift ; **faire cadeau de**, to make a gift of.

poli, polite ; **poliment**, politely ; **la politesse**, politeness.

impoli, impolite, **rude**.

courtois, courteous.

visiter, to visit ; **le visiteur**, *f.* **la visiteuse**, visitor ; **la visite**, visit ; **rendre visite à**, to visit, to call on, *e.g.* je leur ai rendu visite ; **aller en visite**, to go on a visit ; **faire une visite à**, to pay a visit to.

inviter, to invite ; **un invité**,

guest ; **un hôte**, host *or* guest.
accueillir (**cueillir**), to receive, to welcome ; **un accueil**, welcome, reception ; **la bienvenue**, welcome.
saluer, to greet, to acknowledge, to bow to.
présenter, to introduce.
s' incliner, to bow.
embrasser, to kiss ; **le baiser**, kiss.
donner (**serrer**) **la main à**, to shake hands with, *e.g.* **il serra la main au docteur.**
remercier, to thank ; **les remerciements** (*m.*), thanks.
féliciter, to congratulate ; **les félicitations**, congratulations.
faire ses adieux, to say good-byé.
prendre congé, to take one's leave.

6. SALUTATIONS. EXCLAMATIONS

bonjour, good-day, good morning, good afternoon.
bonsoir, good evening.
bonne nuit, goodnight.
au revoir, good-bye.
adieu, farewell.
salut! hello!
à bientôt! I will see you soon!
à ce soir! I will see you this evening!
à tout à l'heure! I will see you presently!
s'il vous (**te**) **plaît**, if you please ; please.
je vous en prie! please! (*the imploring "please!", as in "Stop it, please!"*).
merci, thank you ; **merci beaucoup**, thank you very much.
pardon! excuse me! **pardon?** pardon? **je vous demande pardon**, I beg your pardon, (*apology*).
bravo! bravo! well done!
mon Dieu! good heavens!
par exemple! the idea! upon my word!
tiens! (*surprise*) what! well!
tenez! here! look here!
comment! what!
ma foi! upon my word!
à la bonne heure! well and good!
au secours! help!
allons, come now.
voyons, come now ; now then.
hélas! alas!

7. COLLOQUIAL EXPRESSIONS

comment allez-vous? how are you?
je vais bien, I am well.
comment est-il? what is he like?
quel est votre nom? what is your name?

comment vous appelez-vous? what is your name?
je m'appelle Jean, my name is John.
qu'y a-t-il? what is the matter?
qu'avez-vous? what is the matter with you?
à qui est ce chapeau? whose hat is this?
ce chapeau est à moi, this hat is mine.
il est très aimable (gentil, poli) avec moi, he is very pleasant (nice, polite) to me.
venez par ici, voulez-vous? come this way, will you?
je veux bien, I am quite willing.
c'est cela (ça), that is good; that is right.
c'est bien, that is good; that is right.
faites comme chez vous, make yourself at home.
c'est-à-dire, that is to say.
comme cela (ça), like that.
soyez tranquille, don't worry.
c'est entendu, that is understood; very well then.
bien sûr! to be sure! of course!
dites donc! I say!
que c'est joli! how pretty it is!
comment cela se fait-il? how is that? how does that come about?
au contraire, on the contrary; far from it.
quel dommage! what a pity!
cela dépend, that depends.
jamais de la vie, never on your life.
cela ne fait rien, that does not matter.
cela m'est égal, it is all the same to me; I don't mind.
je ne demande pas mieux, I ask for nothing better; I shall be only too pleased.
il n'y a pas de quoi, don't mention it.
cela va sans dire, it goes without saying.
je n'en sais rien, I don't know.
je n'y comprends rien, I can't make it out.
c'est plus fort que moi, I can't help it.

8. SPEECH

le **mot,** word.
la **parole,** word (*stressing the idea of meaning*); speech; **M. Martin prit alors la parole,** Mr. Martin then spoke.
la **conversation,** conversation.
un **entretien,** conversation, talk.
dire (*irr.*), to say, to tell, *e.g.* **je leur dis d'attendre,** I tell them to wait.
parler, to speak, to talk.
se **taire** (*irr.*), to be (become) silent, to say nothing.
causer, to chat.
bavarder, to chatter, to gossip; **bavard,** talkative.
appeler, to call; **s'appeler**

to be called ; **un appel**, call, appeal ; **rappeler**, to recall.

s' adresser à, to address oneself to, to speak to, to apply to.

téléphoner, to telephone.

demander, to ask (for) ; **je demande à la bonne d'apporter un verre**, I ask the maid to bring a glass ; **se demander**, to ask oneself, to wonder ; **la demande**, request.

prier, to beg, to ask, *e.g.* **je les prie de rester.**

répondre (vendre), to answer, to reply, *e.g.* **il répond à ma question** ; **la réponse**, answer, reply.

répliquer, to reply, to retort.

répéter, to repeat.

ajouter, to add.

interrompre (rompre), to interrupt.

prononcer, to pronounce.

murmurer, to murmur, to whisper.

chuchoter, to whisper.

grogner, to grunt, to grumble.

balbutier, to stammer.

9. VERBS RELATING TO THE MATTER OF SPEECH

raconter, to relate, to tell ; **conter**, to relate.

plaisanter, to joke ; **la plaisanterie**, joke.

exprimer, to express.

annoncer, to announce.

admettre (mettre), to admit.

consentir (dormir), to consent.

avouer, to confess ; **un aveu**, confession, admission.

obéir (finir), to obey, *e.g.* **je lui obéis**, I obey him ; **l'obéissance** (*f.*), obedience.

excuser, to excuse ; **s'excuser**, to excuse oneself, to apologize ; **une excuse**, excuse ; **faire des excuses**, to apologize.

discuter, to discuss, to argue.

expliquer, to explain.

assurer, to assure ; **rassurer**, to reassure.

proposer, to propose, to suggest.

questionner, to question.

interroger, to question.

consulter, to consult.

promettre (mettre), to promise, *e.g.* **je leur ai promis d'aller les voir** ; **la promesse**, promise ; **je tiens ma promesse**, I keep my promise.

rendre grâces à, to give thanks to.

prévenir (venir), to warn ; to inform.

avertir (finir), to warn ; **un avertissement**, warning.

permettre (mettre), to permit, to

allow, to enable, *e.g.* je leur permets d'entrer ; la permission, permission ; leave.
refuser, to refuse, *e.g.* je refuse de le croire.
défendre (vendre), to forbid, *e.g.* je lui défends de parler.
persuader, to persuade.
conseiller, to advise, *e.g.* je lui conseille de payer ; **le conseil**, (piece of) advice.
recommander, to recommend, to advise.
engager, to urge, to induce, *e.g.* je les engage à rentrer chez eux.
ordonner, to order, *e.g.* je lui ordonne de sortir.
exiger, to demand.
intervenir (venir), to intervene.

10. THE BODY
(excluding head and face)

le corps, body.
un os, bone.
la chair, flesh.
la peau, skin.
le sang, blood.
le cœur, heart ; **apprendre par cœur**, to learn by heart.
le cadavre, corpse.
la taille, stature ; waist.
la silhouette, (human) form, figure.

grand, tall.
petit (*of people*), short.
gros, *f.* **grosse**, big, stout.
gras, *f.* **grasse**, fat.
mince, slim.
maigre, thin.
fort, strong.

le dos, back.
la poitrine, chest.
une épaule, shoulder ; **hausser les épaules**, to shrug one's shoulders.
le bras, arm.
le coude, elbow.
la main, hand ; **à la main**, in one's hand ; **battre des mains**, to clap ; **manier**, to handle.
le poing, fist ; **le coup de poing**, punch.
le doigt, finger.
le pouce, thumb.
un ongle, finger-nail.
la jambe, leg ; **il court à toutes jambes**, he is running at full speed (*or* as fast as he can).
le genou (*pl.* **-x**), knee ; **à genoux**, on one's knees ; **s'agenouiller**, to kneel down.
le pied, foot ; **à pied**, on foot ; **frapper du pied**, to stamp (one's foot), **marcher sur la pointe des pieds**, to walk on tip-toe.
le talon, heel.

Je lève la main. I raise my hand.

Il se lave les mains. He washes his hands.
Je lui pris la main. I took his (her) hand.

Vous avez les bras forts. You have strong arms.

11. THE BODY: MOVEMENT AND REST

une allure, walk, gait.
la démarche, walk, gait.
le pas, step, pace; **aller au pas**, to go at a walking-pace; **à deux pas**, two steps away, quite close; **à pas de loup**, on tip-toe, with stealthy tread.
bouger, to move, to shift.
marcher, to walk; to go along, to travel.
courir (*irr.*), to run; **accourir**, to run up; **parcourir**, to travel across (*or* through); to glance through (*letter, book, etc.*)
sauter, to jump.
le bond, leap, bound; **bondir** (finir), to bound, to leap.
boiter, to limp.
le geste, gesture.
le signe, sign; **je leur fais signe**, I make a sign to them, I beckon them.
toucher, to touch.
trembler, to tremble.
frissonner, to shiver.

s'asseoir (*irr.*), to sit down; **je m'assieds**, I sit down; **je suis assis**, I am sitting.
prendre place, to take a seat.
se lever, to get up.
se dresser, to get up, to straighten up.
se tenir (*irr.*), to stand; **se tenir debout**, to stand upright; **je suis debout**, I am standing (up).
s'appuyer, to lean (*for support*).
étendre (vendre), to extend, to stretch; **s'étendre**, to stretch oneself out, to lie down; **étendu**, stretched out, lying.
s'allonger, to lie down (*at full length*).
se pencher, to lean (over), to bend.
baisser, to lower; **se baisser**, to stoop (bend) down.
accroupi, crouching, squatting.
tourner, to turn; **il se tourna vers moi**, he turned to me; **se retourner**, to turn (*or* look) round.
se balancer, to sway.
se rouler, to roll (about).

coucher, to sleep, to spend the night, *e.g.* j'ai couché à l'hôtel; **se coucher**, to lie down, to go to bed ; **il est couché**, he is in bed.

se reposer, to rest; **le repos**, rest.

dormir (*irr.*), to sleep ; **s'endormir**, to go to sleep.

le sommeil, sleep ; **j'ai sommeil**, I feel sleepy ; **sommeiller**, to slumber, to doze.

le somme, nap, *e.g.* il faisait un petit somme.

éveiller *or* **réveiller**, to waken ; to rouse ; **s'éveiller, se réveiller**, to wake up, to awake ; **se réveiller en sursaut**, to wake up with a start.

12. INTRANSITIVE VERBS OF MOTION NORMALLY CONJUGATED WITH *ÊTRE*

aller (*with* être), to go ; **s'en aller**, to go away ; **les allées et venues**, comings and goings.

venir (*with* être), to come ; **il vient de sortir**, he has just gone out ; **il venait de sortir**, he had just gone out ; **revenir** (*with* être), to come back, to return ; **devenir** (*with* être), to become ; **qu'est-il devenu?** what has become of him? **parvenir** (*with* être), to reach ; to succeed, to manage, *e.g.* il parvint à s'échapper.

arriver (*with* être), to arrive.

partir (*with* être), to depart, to set out, *e.g.* il est parti pour le Canada ; **le départ**, departure.

retourner (*with* être), to go back, to return ; **le retour**, return ; **à mon retour**, on my return ; **il est de retour**, he is back.

entrer (*with* être), to enter, to go in, *e.g.* il est entré dans la maison ; **rentrer** (*with* être), to go (come) home, to re-enter ; **rentrer** (*with* avoir), to bring (take) in, *e.g.* j'ai rentré les bicyclettes.

sortir (*with* être), to go (come) out ; **sortir** (*with* avoir), to take out, *e.g.* elle a sorti son mouchoir.

monter (*with* être), to go (come) up ; **monter** (*with* avoir), to take (bring) up, *e.g.* j'ai monté les bagages.

descendre (*with* être), to descend, to go (come) down ; **descendre** (*with* avoir), to take (bring) down, *e.g.* j'ai descendu les bagages.

tomber (*with* être), to fall.

13. OTHER VERBS OF MOTION

(all conjugated with *avoir*, except the reflexive verbs)

passer, to pass; **je passe devant l'église,** I pass the church; **se passer,** to happen; **se passer de quelque chose,** to do without something; **dépasser,** to go past (beyond), to exceed.

approcher, to approach, to draw near, *e.g.* nous approchons de la ville; approcher (*used transitively*), to bring close, *e.g.* approchez votre chaise; **s'approcher,** to approach, *e.g.* il s'approcha de la maison.

(s') avancer, to advance, to come forward.

reculer, to recoil, to move back.

grimper, to climb, *e.g.* il grimpa dans (*or* sur) un arbre.

glisser, to slide, to glide, to slip; **se glisser dans,** to creep into; **glissant,** slippery.

échapper, to escape, *e.g.* il échappa à la mort; **s'échapper de,** to escape from (=*out of*), *e.g.* il s'échappa de sa prison.

pénétrer, to penetrate, to enter, *e.g.* il pénétra dans la cour.

errer, to wander.

rôder, to roam, to prowl.

flâner, to stroll, to idle about.

se rendre (vendre), to surrender; to go, *e.g.* **il se rendit à son bureau,** he went to his office.

se diriger vers, to go towards, to make for, *e.g.* il se dirigea vers la porte.

s' engager dans, to start along, *e.g.* il s'engagea dans une petite rue.

s' élancer, to dash forward.

se précipiter, to rush.

s' éloigner, to move (*or* walk) away.

s' égarer, to stray, to be lost.

s' écrouler, to fall down, to collapse.

faire demi-tour, to turn about.

se mettre en route (en marche), to start off.

Ils l'acclamèrent sur son passage. They cheered him as he went by.

14. THE BODY: HEAD AND FACE

la tête, head; **hocher la tête,** to shake (*or* nod) one's head; **détourner la tête,** to turn one's head away, to look away; **en tête,** at the head, in front.

le cou, neck ; **il se jeta au cou de sa mère**, he threw his arms round his mother's neck.

la gorge, throat ; **ronfler**, to snore ; **tousser**, to cough ; **cracher**, to spit.

le visage, face.

la figure, face.

le teint, complexion.

la ride, wrinkle ; **ridé**, wrinkled.

les cheveux (*m.*), hair ; **blond**, fair ; **brun**, brown, dark ; **roux**, *f.* **rousse**, auburn, "red" ; **grisonnant**, greying ; **le peigne**, comb.

la barbe, beard.

le front, forehead, brow.

la joue, cheek.

le nez, nose ; **se moucher**, to blow one's nose ; **le mouchoir**, handkerchief ; **flairer**, to scent, to smell (out).

la bouche, mouth ; **la bouchée**, mouthful.

la lèvre, lip.

la dent, tooth ; **le mal aux dents**, tooth-ache ; **la brosse à dents**, tooth-brush; **le dentiste**, dentist.

La dame aux cheveux blancs. The lady with white hair.

beau (**bel** before a vowel), *f.* **belle**, beautiful, handsome.

joli, pretty.

laid, ugly.

pâle, pale ; **pâlir** (finir), to grow pale, to go white.

15. EYES AND SIGHT

un œil, *pl.* **des yeux**, eye ; **un coup d'œil**, glance ; **en un clin d'œil**, in the twinkling of an eye ; **il ouvrit de grands (gros) yeux**, he opened his eyes wide ; **les lunettes** (*f.*), spectacles ; **aveugle**, blind ; **éblouir** (finir), to dazzle.

la paupière, eyelid.

le cil, eyelash.

le sourcil, eyebrow.

voir (*irr.*), to see ; **revoir**, to see again ; **la vue**, sight ; view.

regarder, to look (at) ; **le regard**, look, glance ; **il les suivit du regard**, he kept his eyes on them, he watched them ; **il me regarda fixement**, he stared at me.

apercevoir (recevoir), to perceive, to catch sight of.

distinguer, to distinguish, to make out.

observer, to observe.

guetter, to watch for.
paraître (connaître), to appear; **apparaître**, to appear; **disparaître**, to disappear.

se montrer, to show oneself, to appear.

Elle a l'air contente. She looks pleased.

16. HEARING AND SOUND

une oreille, ear; **prêter l'oreille**, to listen (carefully).
entendre (vendre), to hear; **j'ai entendu dire que...** I have heard that...; **j'ai entendu parler de lui**, I have heard of him; **ils s'entendent**, they agree; **un bruit se fit entendre**, a sound was heard; **bien entendu**, of course.
écouter, to listen (to).
sourd, deaf; muffled.
le bruit, noise; **à grand bruit**, noisily; **bruyant**, noisy.

le son, sound; **sonner**, to ring.
le ton, tone.
le silence, silence; **silencieux**, silent.
muet, *f.* **muette**, dumb, mute.
retentir (finir), to resound, to ring out.
siffler, to whistle; **le sifflet**, whistle.
grincer, to grate, to creak.

Il fit claquer la porte. He slammed the door.

17. BREATH. VOICE. OUTWARD EXPRESSION OF FEELING

respirer, to breathe.
l' haleine (*f.*), breath; **reprendre haleine**, to regain one's breath; **hors d'haleine**, out of breath.
le souffle, breath; **souffler**, to breathe (hard), to blow; **essoufflé**, out of breath.
suer, to sweat; **la sueur**, sweat; **en sueur**, sweating.

la voix, voice; **à haute voix**, aloud; **à voix basse**, quietly; **chanter**, to sing; **hurler**, to howl, to yell.
le cri, shout, cry; **pousser un cri**, to utter a cry; **crier**, to shout, to cry out; **s'écrier**, to exclaim.
rire (*irr.*), to laugh; **rire de bon cœur**, to laugh heartily;

ils riaient à mes dépens, they were laughing at my expense ; **le rire,** laughter ; **éclater de rire,** to burst out laughing.

sourire (rire), to smile ; **le sourire,** smile.

pleurer, to weep, to cry ; **les pleurs** (*m.*), weeping, tears ; **en pleurs,** in tears, weeping.

la larme, tear ; **fondre en larmes,** to burst into tears.

le soupir, sigh ; **soupirer,** to sigh.

le sanglot, sob ; **sangloter,** to sob.

gémir (finir), to moan, to groan ; **le gémissement,** moan, groan.

18. PERSONAL TOILET

le bain, bath, bathe ; **prendre un bain,** to have a bath ; **la salle de bains,** bath-room.

la douche, shower(-bath) ; **prendre une douche,** to have a shower.

la toilette, toilet, dressing ; lavatory ; **faire sa toilette,** to wash and get ready.

laver, to wash.

essuyer, to wipe.

se raser, to shave.

le lavabo, wash-basin.

le robinet, tap.

le savon, soap.

la serviette de toilette, towel.

un essuie-mains, towel.

se maquiller, to make up (*with cosmetics*) ; **le maquillage,** make-up.

la poudre, powder.

le talc, talcum powder.

19. HEALTH AND SICKNESS

la santé, health ; **sain,** healthy; wholesome.

la mine, look, appearance (*as regards health*) ; **il avait bonne mine,** he looked well.

se porter, to be (*in health*) ; **elle se porte bien,** *or* **elle va bien,** she is well ; **elle n'est pas bien portante,** she is not in good health.

malade, ill, sick ; **le (la) malade,** sick person, patient ; **la maladie,** illness.

le mal, complaint, ache ; hurt, harm ; **j'ai mal à la tête,** I have a head-ache ; **cela me fait mal,** that hurts me ; **il s'est fait mal,** he has hurt himself.

la douleur, pain ; **une douleur aiguë,** a sharp pain ; **douloureux,** painful.

souffrir (ouvrir), to suffer ; **la souffrance,** suffering.

enrhumé, having a cold ; **je suis enrhumé,** I have a cold.

évanoui, fainting, having fainted.
le médecin, doctor.
un état, state, condition.
soigner, to attend to, to look after (*medically*), *e.g.* **le docteur soigne ses malades.**
soulager, to ease, to relieve.
guérir (finir), to cure, to heal.
un hôpital, hospital.

20. CLOTHES
(general)

les habits (*m.*), clothes.
les vêtements (*m.*), clothes.
la tenue, dress (*general*), get-up.
le haillon, rag, tatter; **en haillons,** in rags.
le linge, linen (*personal and household*).
la poche, pocket.
la manche, sleeve.
la paire, pair.
le gant, glove.
le mouchoir, handkerchief.
le cache-nez, scarf.
le chapeau, hat; **le voile,** veil.
la casquette, peaked cap.
le soulier, shoe; **les souliers jaunes,** brown shoes.
le cuir, leather.
la semelle, sole (*of shoe*).
la pantoufle, slipper.
les espadrilles (*f.*), canvas shoes with rope soles.
cirer, to clean *or* polish (*shoes*).
s'habiller, to dress (oneself); **habillé,** dressed; **vêtu,** dressed, clad.
se déshabiller, to undress (oneself).
ôter, to take off.
brosser, to brush.
nu, bare, naked.

21. WOMEN'S CLOTHES
DRESSMAKING

la robe, dress, frock; **la robe de chambre,** dressing-gown.
le soutien-gorge, brassière.
le porte-jarretelles, suspender belt.
la jupe, skirt.
le tailleur, suit.
le tablier, apron.
le manteau, (*woman's*) coat.
le foulard, scarf.
le bas, stocking.
le collant, tights.
coudre (*irr.*), to sew.
la couture, dressmaking; **le couturier,** *f.* **la couturière,** dressmaker.
raccommoder, to mend.
une aiguille, needle; *also* hand (*of watch or clock*).
les ciseaux (*m.*), scissors.
une épingle, pin.

le bouton, button.
une étoffe, stuff, material.
la laine, wool ; **tricoter**, to knit.
la soie, silk.
le velours, velvet.
la toile, linen (*cloth*) ; canvas.
la doublure, lining.
le ruban, ribbon.
la dentelle, lace.

22. MEN'S CLOTHES

le tailleur, tailor.
le complet, suit.
le faux-col, collar.
la cravate, tie.
la chemise, shirt.
le gilet, waistcoat.
le pull(over), pullover.
le veston, jacket.
la veste, short jacket (*of waiters, pages, etc.*).
le pardessus, overcoat.
la blouse, smock, overall.
le blouson, leather jacket.
la chaussette, sock.
le caleçon, (under)pants.
le pantalon, (*long*) trousers.
la culotte, (*short*) trousers.
le short, shorts.
la ceinture, belt.
le suède, suede.

23. COLOURS

la couleur, colour.
blanc, *f.* **blanche**, white ; **blanchir** (finir), to whiten.
noir, black ; **noircir** (finir), to blacken.
rouge, red ; **rougir** (finir), to redden, to blush.
bleu, *pl.* **bleus**, blue.
jaune, yellow.
brun, brown ; dark (*person*).
vert, green.
rose, pink.
gris, grey.
clair, light.
foncé, dark (*colour*).
sombre, dark (*colour*).

24. PERSONAL THINGS

la chose, thing ; **quelque chose de nouveau**, something new.
un objet, object.
un article, article.
le sac à main, handbag.
la montre, watch ; **la montre-bracelet**, wrist-watch.
la chaîne, chain.
le bijou (*pl.* **-x**), jewel.

le collier, necklace.
le bracelet, bracelet.
l' or (*m*.), gold.
l' argent (*m*.), silver ; money.
la bague, ring (*for finger*).
un anneau, ring.
le parapluie, umbrella.
une ombrelle, sunshade.
la canne, walking-stick.
le bâton, (*any*) stick.
le portefeuille, wallet.
le canif, penknife.
le tabac, tobacco ; **fumer**, to smoke.
la cigarette, cigarette.
un étui, cigarette-case.
la pipe, pipe.
un appareil (photographique), camera.
la photographie, photograph.
la caméra, cine-camera.

25. SOME ADJECTIVES

(usually descriptive of objects)

propre, clean, *e.g*. un visage propre ; **propre** (*before the noun*), own, *e.g*. mes propres livres.
sale, dirty.
dur, hard ; **la dureté**, hardness ; harshness.
mou, *f*. **molle**, soft.
solide, solid, firm, strong.
raide, stiff ; steep.
usé, worn out.
plein, full ; **en pleine mer**, in the open sea.
vide, empty ; **vider**, to empty.
creux, hollow.
désert, deserted, *e.g*. les rues étaient désertes.

26. WORDS RELATING TO COMPARISON AND DIFFERENCE

même (*adj*.), same ; **même** (*adv*.), even ; **tout de même**, all the same ; **quand même**, all the same.
semblable, similar, like.
pareil, *f*. **pareille**, like, similar ; such.
meilleur (*adj*.), better ; **mieux** (*adv*.), better.
autre, other ; **nous autres Français**, we French people ; **autrement**, otherwise.
différent, different ; **la différence**, difference.
ordinaire, ordinary ; **extraordinaire**, extraordinary.
rare, rare, scarce ; **rarement**, rarely, seldom.
favori, *f*. **favorite**, favourite.

particulier, particular; peculiar; private; **particulièrement,** particularly.
varié, varied.

chaque, each, *e.g.* chaque homme, chaque femme.

quelque, some, *e.g.* j'ai lu cela dans quelque livre; quelques, some, a few, *e.g.* j'ai vu quelques amis.
la sorte, sort, kind.
une espèce, species; **sort,** kind.

27. THE HOUSE
(general)

la maison, house; **à la maison,** at home.
le logis, house, dwelling; **au logis,** at home.
un appartement, flat, apartment.
la façade, front (*of a building*).
un étage, floor, storey.
le rez-de-chaussée, ground floor.
le toit, roof.
la mansarde, attic.
le mur, wall; escalader un mur, to scale (*or* climb over) a wall.
la muraille, wall.

le (la) **locataire,** tenant; **louer,** to rent; **le loyer,** rent.

le propriétaire, owner.
le (la) **concierge,** caretaker, doorkeeper, janitor.

habiter, to live (in), *e.g.* mon ami habite Rouen.
demeurer, to live, to dwell, *e.g.* il demeure à Rouen; **la demeure.** dwelling
s' installer dans une maison, to settle into a house.

bâtir (finir), to build; **le bâtiment,** building.
construire (conduire), to build, construct.
démolir (finir), to demolish.

28. HOUSEHOLD WORK. SERVANTS

le ménage, household; **la ménagère,** housewife; **faire son ménage,** to do one's housework; **la femme de ménage,** charwoman, daily help; **déménager,** to move house, to remove.
le (la) **domestique,** servant.

la bonne, housemaid.
la femme de chambre, maid.
le balai, broom ; **balayer,** to sweep.
la poussière, dust ; **prendre les poussières,** to dust.
un aspirateur, vacuum cleaner.
le seau, bucket, pail.
nettoyer, to clean.
ranger, to put straight, to tidy up.

29. PARTS OF THE HOUSE

la pièce, (*any*) room.
la salle, room ; **la salle à manger,** dining-room ; **la salle de bains,** bathroom.
le salon, drawing-room, lounge.
la chambre (à coucher), bedroom.
la cuisine, kitchen ; **la cuisinière,** cook.
le cabinet de travail, study.
le vestibule, entrance hall.
la cave, cellar.
le plancher, (*boarded*) floor.
le parquet, (*block*) floor.
le plafond, ceiling.
un escalier, stairs, staircase.
la marche, stair, step.
un ascenseur, lift, elevator.
le couloir, corridor, passage.
le palier, landing.
le cabinet *or* **la toilette,** toilet, W.C.
la porte, door ; gate ; **la porte d'entrée,** front door, street door ; **nous l'avons mis à la porte,** we turned him out.
le seuil, threshold, door-step.
la sonnette, bell.
la fenêtre, window ; **il regarde par la fenêtre,** he is looking out of the window.
la vitre, window-pane.
le carreau, window-pane ; tile.
le volet, shutter.
le contrevent, shutter.
le rideau, curtain.
la clef, key ; **fermer à clef,** to lock
la serrure, lock.
le verrou, bolt.
la grille, (iron) gate.
le portail, big doors, doorway.
la cour, yard.
un écriteau, notice-board (*sale-board*, etc.).
Ma chambre donne sur la rue. My bedroom overlooks the street.

30. FURNITURE

le meuble, piece of furniture ; **les meubles,** furniture ; **meublé,** furnished.
la table, table.
la chaise, chair.
le fauteuil, armchair.
le coussin, cushion.
le tapis, carpet ; table-cover.
une armoire, cupboard.
le buffet, sideboard.

le bureau, desk ; office.
le **tiroir, drawer.**
le **miroir,** mirror.
la glace, mirror ; *also* ice.
la pendule, clock ; **remonter la pendule, to wind up the clock.**
le **vase, vase.**
le **divan,** couch, sofa, divan.
le **lit, bed.**
le **chevet, bed-head** ; **un livre de chevet, bed-side book.**
le **drap, sheet.**
la **couverture, blanket.**
confortable, comfortable.

31. THE HOUSE: HEAT AND LIGHT

la cheminée, chimney ; fire-place, mantelpiece.
le foyer, hearth ; *sometimes* home.
le feu, fire ; **au coin du feu,** at (by) the fire-side ; **allumer du feu,** to light a fire.
le **chauffage central,** central heating.
le radiateur, radiator.
une allumette, match.
le charbon, coal.
le bois, wood.
la fumée, smoke.
une étincelle, spark.
un incendie, big fire, **conflagration.**
le pompier, fireman.
la lumière, light.
la lueur, glimmer, **glow.**
la lampe, lamp.
la bougie, candle.
l' électricité (*f.*), electricity.
allumer, to light.
brûler, to burn.
éclairer, to light up, to illumine.
éteindre (craindre), **to extinguish,** to put out ; **le feu s'éteint,** the **fire** goes out.
une ampoule électrique, electric bulb.

32. HOTEL. RESTAURANT. CAFÉ

un hôtel, hotel ; **un hôtelier,** hotel-keeper.
une auberge, inn ; **un aubergiste,** inn-keeper.
la pension, boarding-house ; board ; **prendre pension,** to board ; **le (la) pensionnaire,** boarder.
le restaurant, restaurant.
le repas, meal.
le menu, menu.
le petit déjeuner, breakfast.
le déjeuner, lunch, mid-day meal ; **déjeuner,** to have breakfast ***or*** to have lunch.
le dîner, dinner ; **dîner,** to dine, to have dinner.
le souper, supper.
le banquet, (*ceremonial*) **dinner.**

le café, café ; coffee.
la terrasse, terrace, outdoor part of a café.
le garçon, waiter.
la serveuse, waitress.
la consommation, drink (*in a café*).
l' addition (*f.*), total.
la note, (*hotel*) bill.
le pourboire, tip.

33. PREPARATION AND CONSUMPTION OF FOOD

mettre la table, to lay the table ; **se mettre à table**, to sit down at table, to sit down for the meal.
la nappe, table-cloth.
le couvert, place at table, cover ; **mettre le couvert**, to lay the table.
une assiette, plate.
le verre, glass.
le couteau, knife.
la fourchette, fork.
la cuiller, spoon.
la corbeille, basket (*for bread on table, etc.*).
le plateau, tray.
la vaisselle, crockery, crocks ; **faire la vaisselle**, to wash up ; **le lave-vaisselle**, dish washer.
le pot, pot.
la casserole, saucepan.
le couvercle, lid.
une écuelle, bowl, basin.
la marmite, stew-pot.
le four, oven.
le réfrigérateur, refrigerator
la cuisinière à gaz, gas cooker.
la cuisinière électrique, electric cooker.

34. FOOD

(general)

la nourriture, food ; **nourrir** (finir), to feed.
la faim, hunger ; **j'ai faim**, I am hungry ; **mourir de faim**, to die of hunger, to starve ; **affamé**, hungry, famished, starving.
l' appétit, appetite ; **manger de bon appétit**, to eat heartily.
le goût, taste ; **goûter**, to taste; **le goûter**, afternoon snack.
la digestion, digestion.
le plat, dish.
le dessert, dessert.
manger, to eat ; **j'ai donné à manger aux chats**, I have fed the cats.
mordre (vendre), to bite.
dévorer, to devour.
avaler, to swallow.
gourmand, greedy ; **le gourmand**, glutton.
le gourmet, expert in food.

35. FOOD: MEATS, Etc.

la viande, meat.
le bifteck, steak.
le gigot, leg of lamb.
la côtelette, chop.
le jambon, ham.
le lard *or* **le bacon**, bacon.
la saucisse, (*small*) sausage.
le saucisson, dinner-sausage.
un œuf, egg.
une omelette, omelette.
le poisson, fish.
une huître, oyster.
les fruits de mer, shell-fish.
le potage, (thin) soup.
la soupe, soup; **la soupière**, soup-tureen.

le sel, salt.
le poivre, pepper.
la moutarde, mustard.
le vinaigre, vinegar.

cuit, cooked.
rôtir (finir), to roast; **le rôti**, roast (meat).

36. FOOD: VEGETABLES

le légume, vegetable.
la pomme de terre (*pl.* **les pommes de terre**), potato.
le chou (*pl.* **-x**), cabbage.
le chou-fleur, cauliflower.
le haricot, bean; **le haricot vert**, French bean.
les petits pois (*m.*), peas.
la carotte, carrot.
un oignon, onion.
la laitue, lettuce.
le radis, radish.
la salade, salad.
le cresson, watercress.

37. FOOD: FRUITS

le fruit, fruit.
le verger, orchard.
la pomme, apple; **le pommier**, apple-tree.
la poire, pear; **le poirier**, pear-tree.
la prune, plum; **le prunier**, plum-tree.
la pêche, peach; **le pêcher**, peach-tree.
le raisin, grapes; **la grappe**, bunch; **la vigne**, vine, vineyard.
la cerise, cherry; **le cerisier**, cherry-tree.
la fraise, strawberry.
la banane, banana.
une orange, orange.
le citron, lemon.
la tomate, tomato.

mûr, ripe; **mûrir** (finir), to ripen.
cueillir (*irr.*), to gather, to pick.
croquer une pomme, to munch an apple.

38. FOOD: BREAD, Etc. SWEET THINGS

le pain, bread; loaf; **le petit pain**, bread roll.
la baguette, stick of bread.
la tartine, slice of bread (*with butter or jam*).
la tranche, slice (*of anything*).
la croûte, crust.
la miette, crumb.
le beurre, butter.
le fromage, cheese.
la farine, flour.
le gâteau, cake.
le sucre, sugar; **le sucrier**, sugar-basin; **sucré**, sweet (*to the taste*).
la confiture *or* **les confitures**, jam.
le bonbon, sweet.
le chocolat, chocolate.
la glace, ice; ice-cream.

39. DRINKS

l' eau (*f.*), water; **l'eau tiède**, luke-warm water; **l'eau bouillante**, boiling water; **l'eau courante**, running water.
le café, coffee; café; **la cafetière**, coffee-pot.
le thé, tea; **la théière**, tea-pot.
le lait, milk.
la crème, cream.
le vin, wine.
le cidre, cider.
la bière, beer.
la limonade, lemonade.
le jus de fruit, fruit juice.
la boisson, drink, liquor.
la tasse, cup.
la soucoupe, saucer.
le verre, glass.
la bouteille, bottle.
le bouchon, cork; **le tire-bouchon**, cork-screw.
le tonneau, barrel.
la soif, thirst; **j'ai soif**, I am thirsty.
boire (*irr.*), to drink.
verser, to pour (out).

40. THE TOWN

la ville, town, city; **nous allons en ville**, we are going to (into) town.
le quartier, quarter, district.
le faubourg, outlying quarter.
la banlieue, suburbs.
les environs (*m.*), surroundings.
les alentours, surroundings.
la rue, street; **la ruelle**, narrow street, alley-way.
la chaussée, roadway.
le pavé, paved roadway, cobble-stones.
le trottoir, pavement.

le boulevard, boulevard.
le carrefour, crossroads.
la place, square, open space.
le réverbère, street-lamp.

un édifice, building.
un immeuble, (large) building (*offices, flats, etc.*).
le monument, monument.
le palais, palace.

l' hôtel de ville, Town Hall.
le maire, mayor.

un habitant, inhabitant.
le citoyen, citizen.
un agent de police, police constable.
la tournée, beat, round.
le commissaire, police superintendent.
le gardien, keeper (*of monuments, parks, etc.*).
une affiche, poster, notice.
public *f.* publique, public.
principal, principal, main, chief.

41. SHOPS

le magasin, (*large*) shop, store.
le supermarché, supermarket.
la boutique, (*small*) shop.
le marchand, *f.* la marchande, shopkeeper, trader ; la marchandise, goods.
le commerce, trade.
le client, *f.* la cliente, customer.
le marché, market ; la place du marché, market-place.
la foire, (trade) fair.
un épicier, grocer ; une épicerie, grocer's shop.
le boucher, butcher ; la boucherie, butcher's shop.
le boulanger, baker ; la boulangerie, baker's shop.
la pâtisserie, pastry-cook's, confectioner's.
le fruitier, fruiterer.
le marchand de légumes, greengrocer.
le pharmacien, chemist ; la pharmacie, chemist's shop.

le libraire, bookseller ; la librairie, book-shop.
le coiffeur, hairdresser.
le cordonnier, shoe-repairer.

le comptoir, counter.
la caisse, till ; cash-desk.
la vitrine, (shop) window.
le panier, basket.
le paquet, packet, package, parcel.
la boîte, box, tin.
le carton, cardboard ; cardboard box.

Je fais des emplettes. I make some purchases ; I do some shopping.
Je fais des commissions. I go some errands.
Je fais des courses. I make some calls.
3 francs le kilo (le mètre, etc.). 3 francs a kilo (a metre, etc.).

42. MONEY

l' argent (*m.*), money.

la monnaie, change ; **le porte-monnaie**, purse.

la bourse, purse ; *also* scholarship.

la somme, sum (*of money*).

le chiffre, figure, amount.

la pièce, coin.

le billet, bank-note, *e.g.* un billet de dix francs.

le franc, franc.

le sou, sou (*five-centimes*).

le prix, price ; **à tout prix**, at all costs, at any price.

cher, *f.* **chère**, dear ; **peu cher**, cheap.

bon marché (*invariable*), cheap.

précieux, precious.

riche, rich ; **enrichir** (finir), to enrich.

pauvre, poor ; **la pauvreté**, poverty.

misérable, wretched ; **la misère**, dire poverty.

avare, mean, miserly.

gagner, to gain, to earn ; to win.

dépenser, to spend ; **la dépense**, expense, expenditure.

acheter, to buy ; **un achat**, purchase.

vendre, to sell ; **la vente**, sale.

coûter, to cost ; **coûter cher**, to cost dear ; **coûteux**, costly, expensive.

compter, to count, to reckon.

payer, to pay (for), *e.g.* **j'ai payé la marchandise**, I have paid for the goods.

régler, to settle (*e.g. a bill*) ; **le règlement**, rule, regulation.

valoir (*irr.*), to be worth.

prêter, to lend.

emprunter, to borrow, *e.g.* **j'ai emprunté 10 francs à mon frère**, I borrowed 10 francs from my brother.

économiser, to save ; **mes économies**, my savings.

Il a fait fortune. He has made a fortune.

Je n'ai pas les moyens de le faire. I have not the means to do it ; I cannot afford to do it.

43. GARDENS. PARKS

le jardin, garden ; **le jardin public**, public garden, park ; **le jardin potager**, kitchen garden ; **le jardinier**, gardener.

le parc, park.

une allée, path, drive, walk.

le banc, seat.

le siège, seat.

l' herbe (*f.*), grass.

le gazon, turf, greensward.
la pelouse, lawn.
la plante, plant; **planter**, to plant.
pousser, to grow, *e.g.* les plantes poussent.
la fleur, flower.
la tige, stem, stalk.
le parfum, scent, smell.
la plate-bande, *pl.* **les plates-bandes**, flower-bed.
le bassin, (*ornamental*) pond.
le cadran solaire, sundial.
la bêche, spade.
le râteau, rake.
la brouette, wheelbarrow.

le passant, passer-by.
le promeneur, person out walking, stroller.
la promenade, walk; trip; **faire une promenade**, to go for a walk (trip); **se promener**, to walk (*for pleasure*).

44. WORK

le travail, work; **travailler**, to work; **il se mit au travail** (**à l'œuvre**), he set to work.
la besogne, (hard) work.
la tâche, task; **tâcher**, to try, *e.g.* il tâcha d'ouvrir la porte.
le fardeau, burden.
une œuvre, work (*literary or artistic—novel, opera, etc.*)
le métier, trade, occupation.
un emploi, job.
le traitement, salary, pay.
les affaires (*f.*), business.
occupé, busy.

une usine, factory.
la fabrique, factory; **le fabricant**, manufacturer.
le patron, boss, employer.
le personnel, staff, personnel.
un ouvrier, workman.
le maçon, stonemason, bricklayer.
un outil, tool.
le marteau, hammer; *also* door-knocker.
le clou, nail.
la planche, plank, board.
une échelle, ladder.
la corde, rope.
la ficelle, string.
la pelle, shovel.
le fer, iron.
l' acier (*m.*), steel.

45. SCHOOL

une école, school; **un écolier**, schoolboy; **une écolière**, schoolgirl.
le lycée, central high school.
le collège, high school.
la récréation, play-time, "break".
les vacances (*f.*), holidays; **les**

grandes vacances, summer holidays; **la colonie de vacances,** holiday camp.

le congé, (*short*) holiday; leave; **un jour de congé,** a day's holiday; **nous avons congé le jeudi,** we have a holiday (day off) on Thursday(s); **prendre congé,** to take one's leave.

la rentrée, return to school.

le maître, master; **la maîtresse,** mistress.

le professeur, master, teacher.

un instituteur, *f.* **une institutrice,** (*primary*) school teacher.

le directeur, headmaster.

un(e) **élève,** pupil, student.

la classe, class; **la salle de classe,** classroom.

la leçon, lesson.

les études (*f.*), studies; **étudier,** to study; **un**(e) **étudiant**(e), student.

un examen, examination.

la composition, composition; test.

les devoirs (*m.*), homework, preparation.

la faute, fault, mistake; **ce n'est pas ma faute,** it is not my fault.

une expression, expression.

l' attention (*f.*), attention; **faire attention,** to pay attention; **attention!** be careful! look out! **attentivement,** attentively.

la liste, list.

le pupitre, desk.

la chaire, master's (mistress's) desk.

le tableau noir, blackboard.

la craie, chalk.

le livre, book; **le livre d'occasion,** second-hand book.

le papier, paper.

le (**papier**) **buvard,** blotting-paper.

le cahier, exercise book.

le carnet, (small) note-book.

la marge, margin.

le porte-plume, pen; **le bec de plume,** nib.

le stylo, fountain-pen.

le bic, biro.

l' encre (*f.*), ink; **un encrier,** inkwell, inkpot.

la tache, blot, spot.

le crayon, pencil; **le dessin,** drawing; **dessiner,** to draw.

une image, picture.

la gomme, rubber.

la règle, ruler.

enseigner, to teach; **l'enseignement** (*m.*), teaching; **se renseigner,** to make enquiries, to get information; **un renseignement,** enquiry; piece of information.

instruire (**conduire**), to instruct.

apprendre (**prendre**), to learn; to teach.

traduire (**conduire**), to translate.

écrire (*irr.*), to write; l'écriture (*f.*), writing; **décrire** (écrire), to describe; **la description, description.** **imprimer, to print.**

46. CORRESPONDENCE

la lettre, letter; **mettre une lettre à la poste**; to post a letter.
la boîte aux lettres, letter-box; **jeter une lettre à la boîte,** to post a letter.
une enveloppe, envelope.
une adresse, address.
le timbre-poste, *pl.* **les timbres-poste,** postage-stamp.
la carte, card; **la carte postale,** postcard.
la dépêche, telegram.
le courrier, mail, correspondence.
la poste, post; **l'hôtel des postes,** General Post Office; **le bureau de poste,** (*small*) post-office.
le facteur, postman.
la nouvelle, (piece of) news; **des nouvelles,** news; **avez-vous des nouvelles de Jean?** have you any news of John? have you heard from John?
le message, message.
le messager, messenger.

47. READING

lire (*irr.*), to read; **relire,** to re-read; **la lecture,** reading; **le lecteur,** *f.* **la lectrice,** reader.
une histoire, story; history.
le roman, novel; **le roman policier,** detective story.
le conte, short story.
le titre, title.
un auteur, author.
la bibliothèque, library; book-case.
le mot, word.
la ligne, line.
le journal, newspaper.
le rapport, report.
le discours, speech.
un article de fond, leading article.

48. GAMES. PASTIMES

amuser, to amuse; s'amuser, to enjoy oneself; **je me suis bien amusé,** I had a good time; **amusant,** amusing.
le jeu (*pl.* **-x**), **game.**
le sportif, devotee of outdoor games.

jouer, to play; **jouer au tennis (au football, etc.)**, to play tennis (football, etc.); **jouer du violon (du piano)**, to play the violin (the piano).

le jouet, toy.

le joujou (*pl.* -x), plaything.

la poupée, doll.

la balle, ball (*tennis, golf, etc.*).

le ballon, large ball, football; *also* balloon.

la boule, ball (=*something round, e.g. snowball, ball of paper, etc.*).

une équipe, team.

le stade, stadium, ground.

la piscine, swimming pool.

la tente, tent; **camper**, to camp.

l'auberge (*f*) **de la jeunesse**, youth hostel.

le pique-nique, picnic.

49. ENTERTAINMENTS. THE ARTS

le divertissement, amusement, diversion, entertainment.

la distraction, amusement, entertainment.

le théâtre, theatre; stage; **la pièce de théâtre**, play.

le spectacle, (theatre) show.

la représentation, performance; **représenter**, to represent; to play, to perform (*in the theatre*).

assister (à), to be present (at), *e.g.* j'ai assisté à la première représentation.

applaudir (finir), to applaud.

la scène, stage.

le rôle, part (*in a play*).

le personnage, character (*in a play*).

un acteur, actor; **une actrice**, actress.

la vedette, " star " (*of stage or screen*).

la musique, music; **le musicien**, *f.* **la musicienne**, musician.

le concert, concert.

un instrument, instrument.

le piano, piano.

le violon, violin.

la chanson, song.

le tourne-disque, record-player.

le disque, (gramophone) record.

une émission, broadcast.

les informations (*f.*), (*broadcast*) news.

le cinéma, cinema.

le film, film.

l' écran (*m.*), screen.

la radio, radio.

la télévision, television; **le poste de télévision** *or* **le téléviseur**, television set.

la discothèque, discotheque.

le bal, dance, ball; **danser**, to dance.

la fête, fête, celebration; feast-day (*of the Church*).

le peintre, painter; peindre (craindre), to paint; l'étonnement se peignait sur sa figure, surprise showed in his face.
le tableau, picture.
le cadre, frame.

50. THE CHURCH

la cathédrale, cathedral.
une église, church.
la tour, tower.
le clocher, church tower; la cloche, bell; sonner, to ring.
la flèche, spire; arrow.
une horloge, clock (*on church, etc.*).
le vitrail (*pl.* -aux), stained glass window.
la croix, cross.
le chœur, choir.
le cimetière, cemetery.

le prêtre, priest.
le curé, parish priest; la paroisse, parish; le paroissien, parishioner; le presbytère, parish priest's house.
un abbé, abbot; (*Roman Catholic*) clergyman.
le couvent, convent; la religieuse, nun.
la messe, mass.
une âme, soul.
bénir (finir), to bless.

la fête, feast-day, holiday; un jour de fête, feast-day, public holiday.
(la) Noël, Christmas.
le jour de l'an, New Year's Day; les étrennes (*f.*), New Year's gift.
le mardi gras, Shrove Tuesday.
le vendredi saint, Good Friday.
Pâques (*f.*), Easter.
la Pentecôte, Whitsuntide.
l' Assomption (*f.*), feast of the Assumption (August 15).
la Toussaint, All Saints' Day (November 1).

51. RAILWAY TRAVEL

le voyage, journey; voyager, to travel; le voyageur, traveller, passenger.
le trajet, journey.
la destination, destination.
l' arrivée (*f.*), arrival; à mon arrivée, on my arrival.

le chemin de fer, railway.
la gare, station; le train entre

en gare, the train comes into the station; **le chef de gare,** station master.
l'entrée (*f.*), entrance, entry.
la sortie, exit, way out.
la salle d'attente, waiting-room.
l' indicateur (*m.*), time-table.
l' horaire (*m.*), time-table.
le guichet, ticket-office.
le billet, ticket; **je prends mon billet,** I get my ticket.
le contrôleur, ticket inspector.
un employé, porter.
les bagages (*m.*), luggage; **je fais enregistrer mes bagages,** I have my luggage registered.
la malle, trunk.
la valise, suitcase.
la consigne, luggage-room, cloakroom.

le quai, platform.
le trottoir, platform.
la voie, track.
le passage à niveau, level crossing.

le train, train; **le chef de train,** guard; **un express,** semi-fast train; **le rapide,** fast train, express.
le wagon, railway coach; **le wagon-restaurant,** dining car.
le compartiment, compartment.
la portière, door (*of railway coach or any vehicle*).
la banquette, seat.
le filet, net; luggage rack.

52. MOTOR-CARS. TRAVEL BY ROAD AND AIR

une auto(mobile), motor-car.
la voiture, car *or* vehicle.
le taxi, taxi.
un autobus, bus.
un autocar *or* **un car,** motor-coach.
le camion, lorry, truck.
le chauffeur, chauffeur, driver.
le conducteur, driver.
le garage, garage.
le moteur, engine.
l' essence (*f.*), petrol; **le poste d'essence,** petrol pump.
le pétrole, paraffin.
la roue, wheel.

le pneu, tyre.
la panne, breakdown; **en panne,** broken down.
réparer, to repair.

la circulation, traffic.
les feux (de circulation), traffic lights.
le rond-point, roundabout.
la file (de voitures), line (of cars).
la vitesse, speed; **à toute vitesse,** at full speed.
un accident, accident.
rouler, to roll; **to travel**

along; nous roulions à 100 kilomètres à l'heure, we were travelling at 100 kilometres (=60 *miles approx.*) an hour.

filer, to travel (along) *e.g.* nous filions à toute vitesse.

ralentir (finir), to slow down.

stationner, to park.

faire de l'auto-stop, to hitchhike.

la bicyclette, bicycle; **rouler à bicyclette**, to cycle; **le cycliste**, cyclist.

le vélo, bike.

la motocyclette, motor-cycle.

le fouet, whip, **fouetter**, to whip.

un aéroport, airport.

un avion, aeroplane; **en avion**, by air, **décoller**, to take off (*of planes*); **atterrir** (finir), to land; **un atterrissage**, landing.

53. COUNTRIES. DISTRICTS. FRONTIERS

le monde, world; **le monde entier**, the whole world.

le pays, country.

la capitale, capital.

la province, province.

la région, region, district.

un étranger, *f.* **une étrangère**, foreigner; **étranger** (*adj.*), foreign; **à l'étranger**, abroad.

le compatriote, fellow countryman; **la compatriote**, fellow countrywoman.

la frontière, frontier.

la douane, customs; **le douanier**, customs officer.

le contrebandier, smuggler.

fouiller, to search.

le nord, north.

le sud, south

l'est, east.

l' ouest, west.

54. NAMES OF COUNTRIES. INHABITANTS. LANGUAGES

LE PAYS	LES HABITANTS	LA LANGUE
L'Europe (*f.*)	l'Européen l'Européenne	
La France	le Français la Française	le français
Paris	le Parisien la Parisienne	
La Grande-Bretagne L'Angleterre (*f.*)	l'Anglais l'Anglaise	l'anglais

LE PAYS	LES HABITANTS	LA LANGUE
L'Écosse (*f.*) (*Scotland*)	l'Écossais l'Écossaise	l'anglais
Le Pays de Galles (*Wales*)	le Gallois la Galloise	l'anglais le gallois
L'Irlande (*f.*)	l'Irlandais l'Irlandaise	l'anglais l'erse
L'Amérique (*f.*) Les États-Unis (*m.*)	l'Américain l'Américaine	l'anglais
Le Canada	le Canadien la Canadienne	l'anglais le français
L'Australie (*f.*)	l'Australien l'Australienne	l'anglais
La Nouvelle-Zélande	le Néozélandais la Néozélandaise	l'anglais
L'Afrique du Sud	le Sud-Africain la Sud-Africaine	l'anglais l'africaans
L'Allemagne (*f.*) (*Germany*)	l'Allemand l'Allemande	l'allemand
La Russie	le Russe la Russe	le russe
La Hollande	le Hollandais la Hollandaise	le hollandais
La Belgique	le Belge la Belge	le français le flamand
La Suisse (*Switzerland*)	le Suisse la Suissesse	le français l'allemand
L'Italie (*f.*)	l'Italien l'Italienne	l'italien
L'Espagne (*f.*)	l'Espagnol l'Espagnole	l'espagnol

Nous allons en France. We go to France.
Il est en France. He is in France.
Le Midi de la France. The South of France.
La Méditerranée. The Mediterranean.
La Manche. The English Channel.
Je suis Anglais. I am English. I am an Englishman.
C'est une Française. She is a Frenchwoman.
Ces gens-là parlent français. Those people are speaking French.
Vous parlez bien le français. You speak French well.
Vous connaissez bien le français. You know French well.

55. PEACE AND WAR

la paix, peace ; **paisible**, peaceful.
la guerre, war.
la patrie, fatherland, homeland.
le drapeau, flag.
le tambour, drum.
la lutte, struggle ; **lutter**, to struggle.
la bataille, battle.
le coup, blow, stroke.
une attaque, attack ; **attaquer**, to attack.
la victoire, victory.
la défaite, defeat.
la retraite, retreat ; retirement.

le courage, courage, pluck ; **courageux**, courageous, brave ; **encourager**, to encourage ; **décourager**, to discourage.
brave, brave ; *also* worthy, honest.
le danger, danger ; **dangereux**, dangerous.
l' aide (*f.*), help ; **aider**, to help.
le secours, help ; **au secours!** help!
la sûreté, safety ; **sûr**, sure ; safe ; **sain et sauf**, safe and sound.
libre, free ; **la liberté**, freedom.
le soldat, soldier.
l' uniforme (*m.*), uniform.
la caserne, barracks.
le rang, rank.
un officier, officer.
un ennemi, enemy.
un espion, spy.
le prisonnier, prisoner ; **la prison**, prison.
le fusil, rifle, gun ; **le coup de fusil**, rifle shot, gunshot.
le pistolet, pistol.
une épée, sword.
le poignard, dagger.
la bombe, bomb ; **lancer des bombes sur (une ville)**, to bomb (a city).
le raid aérien, air-raid.
la mitraillette, submachine-gun.
le char (d'assaut), tank.
battre (*irr.*), to beat ; **se battre**, to fight ; **combattre**, to fight ; **abattre**, to strike down.
défendre (vendre), to defend; *also* to forbid.
tuer, to kill.
blesser, to wound ; **la blessure**, wound.
défiler, to file (*or* march) past.
envahir (finir), to invade ; **une invasion**, invasion.
se ruer, to rush.
fuir (*irr.*), to flee ; **s'enfuir**, to flee ; **la fuite**, flight ; **le fugitif**, fugitive.
se réfugier, to take refuge.
s' évader, to escape ; **une évasion**, escape.

56. THE COUNTRYSIDE

la campagne, country(-side) ; **à la campagne,** in the country.
le paysage, landscape.
la plaine, plain.
la montagne, mountain.
la colline, hill.
la pente, slope.
le sommet, summit.
la vallée, valley.

le village, village ; **le villageois,** villager.
le bourg, large village, little country town.
le hameau, hamlet.
le château, castle ; country mansion.
la propriété, estate.
la chaumière, (thatched) cottage.
la cabane, small cottage, hut.
la hutte, hut.
le moulin, mill ; **le meunier,** miller.
la route, road (*in the country*) ; **en route pour,** on the way to.
le chemin, road, way ; **il reprit le chemin du village,** he took the road back to the village ; **rebrousser chemin,** to retrace one's steps, to go back ; **en chemin,** on the way ; **chemin faisant,** on the way.
le sentier, path.

le paysan, peasant, countryman.
la paysanne, peasant woman, countrywoman.
le gendarme, policeman (*country districts*).

57. THE LAND AND THE SOIL

la terre, earth, land, ground ; **à terre,** on land ; ashore ; to the ground ; **par terre,** on (*or* to) the ground ; **enterrer,** to bury.
le terrain, ground, land (= *specific piece of ground or land*).
le sol, soil, ground.
la boue, mud.
la poussière, dust.
la pierre, stone.
le caillou (*pl.* **-x**), pebble.
le trou, hole ; **creuser,** to dig.
la caverne, cave, cavern.
la grotte, cave, grotto.

58. THE FARM

la ferme, farm ; **le fermier,** farmer ; **la fermière,** farmer's wife.
la basse-cour, poultry-yard.
une étable, (cow-) shed.
une écurie, stable.

la charrette, cart.
la grange, barn.
le grenier, loft, granary.
la barrière, (farm) gate.
le champ, (*tilled*) field.
la prairie, meadow.
le pré, (*small*) meadow ; paddock.
le fossé, ditch.
cultiver, to cultivate ; to grow (=*produce*).
labourer, to plough ; **le laboureur**, ploughman ; **la charrue**, plough ; **le sillon**, furrow.
le blé, corn.
la paille, straw.
le foin, hay.
le tracteur, tractor.
la moissonneuse-batteuse, combine harvester.
la récolte, crop.
la moisson, harvest.

59. TREES. SHRUBS

un arbre, tree.
le tronc, trunk.
la racine, root.
la branche, branch.
la feuille, leaf ; **le feuillage**, foliage.
le bois, wood.
la forêt, forest.
la hache, axe.
le chêne, oak.
un orme, elm.
le hêtre, beech.
le peuplier, poplar.
le platane, plane-tree.
le noyer, walnut-tree ; **la noix**, walnut.
le châtaignier, (sweet) chestnut-tree ; **la châtaigne**, (*edible*) chestnut.
le marronnier d'Inde, horse-chestnut tree.
le houx, holly.
le pin, pine.
le sapin, fir-tree.
le saule, willow.
le buisson, bush.
la haie, hedge.
la bruyère, heather ; heath.

60. ANIMALS
(mammals)

un animal (*pl.* **-aux**), animal.
la bête, creature, animal, beast.
la gueule, mouth (*of an animal*).
le poil, hair (*of an animal*).
la patte, foot, paw, leg (*of an animal*) ; **à quatre pattes**, on all fours.
la queue, tail.

le cheval (*pl.* **-aux**), horse ; **à cheval**, on horseback ; **le cavalier**, horseman ; **la selle**, saddle ; **galoper**, to gallop ; **atteler**, to harness ;

un attelage, team (*of horses*).
la jument, mare.
un âne, donkey.
la vache, cow ; **le taureau,** bull ; **le bœuf,** ox, steer ; **le veau,** calf.
le bétail, cattle ; **mugir** (finir), to bellow ; to roar.
le mouton, sheep ; **la brebis,** ewe ; **un agneau,** lamb ; **le troupeau,** flock, herd ; **le berger,** shepherd ; **brouter,** to browse, to graze.
la chèvre, goat.
le cochon, pig.
le chien, dog ; **aboyer,** to bark ; **l'aboiement** (*m.*), bark, barking ; **lécher,** to lick ; **le chenil,** kennel ; **la niche,** kennel.
le chat, cat.
le rat, rat ; **à bon chat bon rat,** tit for tat.
la souris, mouse ; **ronger,** to gnaw.

le chasseur, hunter, sportsman, shooter ; **la chasse,** hunting, shooting ; **chasser,** to hunt, to shoot (*game*).
le gibier, game.
le lapin, rabbit.
le lièvre, hare.
le renard, fox.
le piège, trap, snare.
sauvage, wild.

le lion, lion ; **rugir** (finir), to roar , **le rugissement,** roar.
le loup, wolf.
un ours, bear.
le singe, monkey.

61. BIRDS

la poule, hen ; **le coq,** cock ; **le poulet,** chicken ; **le poulailler,** chicken-house, hen-roost.
le canard, duck.
une oie, goose.
la volaille, poultry.
le dindon, *f.* **la dinde,** turkey.
un oiseau, bird.
le moineau, sparrow.
le rouge-gorge, robin.
une hirondelle, swallow.
le rossignol, nightingale.
le corbeau, crow.
le hibou (*pl.* **-x**), owl.
le perroquet, parrot ; **la cage,** cage.
une aile, wing.
le bec, beak.
le chant, (*birds'*) song.
le nid, nest.
voler, to fly ; **s'envoler,** to fly away, to take wing ; **le vol,** flight.

62. INSECTS

une abeille, bee ; **le miel,** honey.
la guêpe, wasp.
le papillon, butterfly ; **le papillon de nuit,** moth.
la mouche, fly.
la sauterelle, grasshopper.
la libellule, dragon-fly.
la cigale, cicada.
la fourmi, ant.
le grillon, cricket.
une araignée, spider.
la puce, flea.
le ver, worm.
le moustique, mosquito.

63. RIVERS AND LAKES

le fleuve, river (=*great river going down to the sea*).
la rivière, river, stream.
le ruisseau, brook.
la rive, bank.
le bord, edge, bank ; **au bord de la rivière,** on the river bank, by the river ; **border,** to line, to go along by ; **déborder,** to overflow.
le pont, bridge.
couler, to flow.
lo courant, current.
flotter, to float.
le lac, lake.
la mare, pond.
un étang, pool.
la grenouille, frog.
le poisson, fish.
la pêche , fishing; **la canne à pêche,** fishing rod; **pêcher,** to fish; **le pêcheur,** fisherman.
le flotteur, float.
le filet, net.

64. THE SEA

la mer, sea.
un océan, ocean.
l' abîme (*m.*), abyss, deep (sea.)
la marée, tide.
la vague, wave.
les flots (*m.*), waves, waters. (*usually poetical*)
une onde, wave, water. (*usually poetical*)

la côte, coast ; *also* rib ; **côte à côte,** side by side.
le rivage, shore.
la falaise, cliff.
le rocher, rock.
le phare, lighthouse.
la baie, bay.
une île, island.
la plage, beach.
le sable, sand.

se baigner, to bathe ; **le baigneur,** bather ; **le bain,** bath, bathe ; **le maillot de**

bain, swimming-costume; le **caleçon de bain**, swimming-shorts.
nager, to swim.
plonger, to dive.

mouiller, to wet; **mouillé**, wet.
sec, *f.* **sèche**, dry; **sécher**, to dry.

65. BOATS. SHIPPING

le **bateau**, boat.
le **navire**, ship.
le **paquebot**, passenger-ship, liner.
la **passerelle**, (*ship's*) bridge; gangway; footbridge.
la **barque**, fishing-boat.
la **voile**, sail.
le **canot**, rowing-boat.
une **amarre**, mooring-rope.

le **marin**, sailor (*seafaring man of any rank*).
le **matelot**, seaman.

le **port**, port, harbour; **le port de mer**, seaport.
le **passager**, (*ship's*) passenger.
la **traversée**, voyage.
s' **embarquer**, to embark; **débarquer**, to disembark.
le **naufrage**, shipwreck; **faire naufrage**, to be (ship-) wrecked.
le **sauvetage**, rescue.
se **noyer**, to be drowned.
le **canot de sauvetage**, lifeboat.
la **ceinture de sauvetage**, life belt.

66. THE SKY AND THE WEATHER

le **ciel**, *pl.* **les cieux**, sky, heaven.
le **soleil**, sun; **au soleil**, in the sun; **il fait du soleil**, it is sunny; **le soleil se lève**, the sun rises; **le lever du soleil**, sunrise; **le soleil se couche**, the sun sets; **le coucher du soleil**, sunset.
le **rayon**, ray.
l' **aube** (*f.*), daybreak, dawn.
le **point du jour**, daybreak.
la **lune**, moon; **le clair de lune**, moonlight.

une **étoile**, star; **coucher à la belle étoile**, to sleep in the open.
un **astre**, star.

briller, to shine; **brillant**, brilliant.
éclater, to burst; to shine forth; **éclatant**, vivid, brilliant.
clair, bright, light; **la clarté**, brightness, radiance.
sombre, dark; **il fait sombre**, it is dark.

obscur, dark ; **l'obscurité** (*f.*), darkness.
une ombre, shadow, shade ; **à l'ombre**, in the shade.

l' air (*m.*), air ; **en l'air**, in(to) the air.
le nuage, cloud.
la brume, mist.
le brouillard, fog, mist ; **il fait du brouillard**, it is foggy ; **le brouillard se dissipe**, the fog disperses (clears).
la rosée, dew.
la pluie, rain ; **pluvieux**, rainy ; **pleuvoir**, to rain ; **il pleut à verse**, it is raining in torrents.
une averse, heavy shower, downpour ; **tremper**, to soak ; **un abri**, shelter ; **(s')abriter**, to shelter.
la goutte, drop.
la neige, snow ; **il neige**, it snows ; **fondre** (vendre), to melt.
le vent, wind ; **il fait du vent**, it is windy.
la brise, breeze.
la tempête, storm, tempest.
un orage, thunderstorm ; **orageux**, stormy ; **le tonnerre**, thunder ; **le grondement**, rumble ; **l'éclair** (*m.*), lightning.
le temps, time, weather ; **quel temps fait-il?** what is the weather like?
chaud, warm ; **très chaud**, hot ; **il fait chaud**, the weather is warm ; **j'ai chaud**, I am warm ; **l'eau est chaude**, the water is warm ; **la chaleur**, heat.
froid, cold ; **il fait froid**, the weather is cold ; **j'ai froid**, I am cold ; **l'eau est froide**, the water is cold ; **refroidir** (finir), to cool.
frais, *f.* **fraîche**, fresh, cool ; **il fait frais**, it is fresh (chilly) ; **la fraîcheur**, freshness.
la glace, ice ; **glacial**, icy, bitterly cold ; **geler**, to freeze ; **il gèle**, it is freezing ; **la gelée**, frost ; **patiner**, to skate ; **les patins** (*m.*), skates.
Par une nuit glaciale. On a bitterly cold night.
les prévisions météorologiques (*abbr.* **la météo**), weather forecast.

67. TIME

le temps, time ; **à temps**, in time ; **en même temps**, at the same time ; **pendant ce temps**, during this time, meanwhile ; **de temps en temps**, from time to time ; **longtemps**, a long time.

le passé, past; **comme par le passé**, as in the past.
l'avenir (*m.*), future; **à l'avenir**, in the future.
le siècle, century; age.
une époque, period, time.
le séjour, stay (*e.g. at the sea-side*).

un an, year; **une année**, year; **pendant bien des années**, for many years.
le mois, month.
la semaine, week.
le jour, day; **huit jours**, a week; **quinze jours**, a fort-night; **de nos jours**, in our day (time); **au petit jour**, at first light; **la journée**, day (*as in "a busy day"*); **journalier**, daily; **quotidien** (*f.* **-ienne**), daily.
le matin, morning; **de grand** (*or* **bon**) **matin**, early in the morning; **du matin au soir**, from morning till night; **la matinée**, morning (*as in "a busy morning"*).
un(e) après-midi, afternoon.
le soir, evening; **la soirée**, evening (*as in "a pleasant evening"*); party.
la nuit, night; **à la nuit tombante**, at nightfall; **à la tombée de la nuit**, at nightfall; **nuit et jour**, day and night.
une heure, hour; **une demi-heure**, half-an-hour; **un quart d'heure**, quarter of an hour; **quelle heure est-il?** what is the time? **il est 9 heures**, it is nine o'clock; **j'ai 11h. 5**, I make it 11.5; **à quelle heure partez-vous?** at what time do you start? **à 9 heures précises**, at exactly 9 o'clock; **de bonne heure**, early; **à l'heure qu'il est**, at the present time; **tout à l'heure**, presently; just now.
la minute, minute.
la seconde, second.
le moment, moment; while; **pour le moment**, for the moment; **en ce moment**, at present.
un instant, instant; moment; **à l'instant**, at once.

tous les jours (mois, ans), every day (month, year).
trois fois par jour (semaine, mois, etc.), three times a day (week, month, etc.).
le mois (l'an) prochain, next month (year).
le mois (l'an) dernier, last month (year).

68. SEASONS. MONTHS. DAYS

les saisons (*f.*), seasons.
le printemps, spring ; **au printemps**, in spring.
l' été (*m.*), summer ; **en été**, in summer.
l' automne (*m.*), autumn ; **en automne**, in the autumn.
l' hiver (*m.*), winter ; **en hiver**, in winter ; **un hiver rigoureux**, a hard winter.
un jour (soir, nuit) d'hiver, one winter day (evening, night).

les mois (*m.*), months.
janvier (*m.*) **mai** (*m.*).
février (*m.*). **juin** (*m.*).
mars (*m.*). **juillet** (*m.*).
avril (*m.*). **août** (*m.*).
septembre (*m.*). **novembre** (*m.*).
octobre (*m.*). **décembre** (*m.*).

en juin, in June.
au mois de juin, in June.
le premier avril, April 1st.
le deux (le trois, etc.) avril, April 2nd (3rd, etc.).

les jours de la semaine.
lundi (*m.*), Monday.
mardi (*m.*), Tuesday.
mercredi (*m.*), Wednesday.
jeudi (*m.*), Thursday.
vendredi (*m.*), Friday.
samedi (*m.*), Saturday.
dimanche (*m.*), Sunday.

69. ADVERBS OF TIME

aujourd'hui, today.
hier, yesterday ; **hier (au) soir**, yesterday evening.
la veille, the evening (*or* day) before ; the eve.
demain, tomorrow.
le lendemain, morrow, next day ; **le lendemain matin**, next morning.

d'abord, at first, first of all.
puis, next, then.
ensuite, then, afterwards.
alors, then (=*at that time*).
enfin, at last, finally.
au bout de, at the end of, after, *e.g.* **au bout d'un mois**, after a month.

maintenant, now.
or, now (*beginning a new paragraph or a fresh part of a story*).
à présent, now (*the strong* now), *e.g* **que fais-tu à présent?** what are you doing *now*?
tout de suite, at once.
immédiatement, immediately, at once.

aussitôt, at once, forthwith.
bientôt, soon ; **plus tôt**, sooner, earlier ; **si tôt**, so soon, so early ; **trop tôt**, too soon, too early.
déjà, already.
il y a un mois, a month ago.
auparavant, before, *e.g.* quelques mois auparavant.
jadis, formerly, in the old days.
jusque-là, up till then.
souvent, often.
fréquemment, frequently.
toujours, always ; still ; **comme toujours**, as usual.
d'habitude, usually.
d'ordinaire, usually.
sans cesse, without ceasing, all the time.
constamment, constantly.
encore, yet ; still ; again ; **pas encore**, not yet.
de nouveau, afresh, again.
tout à coup, suddenly.
soudain, suddenly.
subitement, suddenly.
vite, quickly.
promptement, promptly, quickly.
tard, late, *e.g.* **je me suis couché tard** ; **en retard**, late (= *after time*), *e.g.* **nous sommes arrivés en retard.**
en avance, before time.

la fois, time, *e.g.* **trois fois par jour**, three times a day ; **quelquefois**, sometimes ; **autrefois**, formerly ; **encore une fois**, once more ; **à la fois**, at the same time ; both ; **parfois**, at times, occasionally ; **chaque fois que** *or* **toutes les fois que**, whenever.

70. ADJECTIVES CONNECTED WITH TIME

nouveau, (**nouvel** *before a vowel*), *f.* **nouvelle**, new, fresh ; **renouveler**, to renew ; **neuf**, *f.* **neuve**, brand-new.
moderne, modern.
actuel, *f.* **actuelle**, present.
récent, recent ; **récemment**, recently.
ancien, *f.* **ancienne**, old, former.
prêt, ready ; **s'apprêter à**, to get ready to, *e.g.* **elle s'apprêta à sortir.**
bref, *f.* **brève**, brief ; **brièvement**, briefly.
lent, slow ; **lentement**, slowly ; **ralentir** (**finir**), to slow down ; **la lenteur**, slowness.
régulier, regular ; **régulièrement**, regularly.

71. VERBS CONNECTED WITH TIME

commencer, to begin, *e.g.* il commence à jouer ; **le commencement**, beginning ; **le début**, start, outset.

se mettre à, to start (begin) to, *e.g.* il se mit à chanter.

continuer, to continue, *e.g.* je continue à leur écrire.

conserver, to preserve, to keep.

garder, to keep.

durer, to last.

rester, to remain ; **il me reste cent francs**, I have 100 francs left, **le reste**, rest, *e.g.* je garderai le reste.

s' écouler, to go by, to elapse , **les années s'écoulèrent**, the years went by.

prolonger, to prolong.

finir, to finish , **nous avons fini de jouer**, we have finished playing ; **tout est bien qui finit bien**, all's well that ends well ; **la fin**, end ; **mettre fin à**, to put an end to.

cesser, to cease, *e.g.* **il cessa de crier**, he stopped shouting.

terminer, to end.

achever, to complete, to finish, *e.g.* il acheva d'écrire la lettre.

attendre (vendre), to await, to wait (for) ; **s'attendre à**, to expect, *e.g.* je m'attendais à vous voir ; **inattendu**, unexpected ; **une attente**, wait ; expectation.

se dépêcher, to hurry, *e.g.* il se dépêcha de descendre.

se hâter, to hasten, *e.g.* il se hâta de s'excuser , **la hâte**, haste ; **en toute hâte**, in all haste.

s' empresser, to hasten, *e.g.* le garçon s'empressa de les servir.

presser, to hasten ; **pressé**, pressed, in a hurry ; **presser le pas**, to quicken one's step, to hurry along.

préparer, to prepare ; **se préparer à**, to prepare to, *e.g.* elle se prépara à sortir.

se disposer à, to get ready to, *e.g.* il se disposa à prendre son café.

précéder, to precede ; **précédent**, preceding, previous, *e.g.* la semaine précédente.

succéder (à), to succeed, to come after, *e.g.* une belle matinée succéda à cette nuit d'orage.

tarder, to delay, to be long, *e.g.* **il ne tardera pas à revenir**, he will soon come back ; **retarder**, to delay, *e.g.* cet incident retarda notre départ ; **le retard**, lateness, delay ; **s'attarder**, to linger.

être sur le point de, to be about to, *e.g.* il était sur le point de protester.

72. QUANTITY

le nombre, number ; **nombreux**, numerous.
le numéro, number (*in a series*), *e.g.* le numéro de sa maison.
le chiffre, figure.
la quantité, quantity.

la part, share ; **prendre part à**, to take part in ; **partager**, to share.
la partie, part, portion ; **faire partie de**, to belong to, *e.g.* il fait partie de notre association.
le morceau, piece, bit.
la moitié, half ; **à moitié** *or* **à demi**, (by) half, *e.g.* à moitié (à demi) mort, half dead.
la plupart, most, *e.g.* la plupart des soldats sont jeunes.
le tas, heap, pile.
le monceau, heap.
en moyenne, on an (the) average.
faute de, for lack of, *e.g.* faute d'argent.

beaucoup, much, many, a lot.
combien, how much, how many.
trop, too much, too many ; too.
tant, so much, so many ; **autant**, as much, as many.
assez, enough ; fairly, rather.
plus, more ; **plus de mille francs**, more than 1000 francs.
moins, less, fewer ; **moins de six mois**, less than six months ; **au moins**, at least.
un peu, a little, *e.g.* un peu de salade ; **peu**, little, few, *e.g.* il y a peu de clients ; **peu à peu**, little by little ; **à peu près**, nearly, about, approximately.
plusieurs, several.
davantage, more (*in comparisons*), *e.g.* j'ai beaucoup de livres ; vous en avez davantage.

augmenter, to increase.
suffire (*irr.*), to suffice ; **suffisant**, sufficient ; **suffisamment**, sufficiently.
consister, to consist, *e.g.* la maison consiste en six pièces.

entier, entire, whole
complet, *f.* **complète**, complete ; **incomplet**, incomplete.
nécessaire, necessary.
indispensable, indispensable.
précis, precise ; **précisément**, precisely.
exact, exact ; punctual ; correct ; **exactement**, exactly.

73. PLACE. DIRECTION. DISTANCE

un endroit, place, spot.

le lieu, place; **au lieu de**, instead of; **avoir lieu**, to take place.

la place, place; room (=*space*); seat (*in a vehicle or place of amusement, etc.*); square (*in a town or village*); **à votre place**, in your place.

la situation, situation; **situé**, situated.

la position, position.

le côté, side; direction; **d'un côté**, on one side; **de l'autre côté**, on the other side; **de tous côtés**, on all sides; **à mes côtés**, at my side; **à côté de**, beside, next to; **du côté de**, in (*or* from) the direction of; **mettre de côté**, to put aside.

la part, direction, quarter; **de la part de vos amis**, from your friends; **quelque part**, somewhere; **nulle part**, nowhere; **d'autre part**, on the other hand.

le coin, corner.

le bout, end; **au bout d'un mois**, at the end of (*or* after) a month; **il en viendra à bout de cette entreprise**, he will carry through (succeed in) this enterprise.

le fond, bottom; back, far end; **au (du) fond de l'eau**, in (from) the depths of the water; **au fond de la salle**, at the back (far end) of the room.

la distance, distance; **à quelque distance**, some distance away; **ce village se trouve à 15 kilomètres d'Orléans**, this village is 15 kilometres from Orleans.

le mètre, metre; **le kilomètre**, kilometre (=*approx. five-eighths of a mile*).

le mille, mile.

la lieue, league (4 *kilometres or approx. two and a half miles*).

l' espace (*m.*), space.

droit, right; **à droite**, on (to) the right; **allez tout droit**, go straight on; **le droit**, right; law.

gauche, left; **à gauche**, on (to) the left.

supérieur, superior; upper, higher.

inférieur, inferior, lower.

proche, near.

voisin, neighbouring.

isolé, isolated, lonely.

ici, here.

là, there; **là-bas**, yonder, over there; **là-haut**, up there; **là-dessus**, thereupon; **çà et là**, here and there.

dedans, in, inside; **là-dedans**, in there.

(en) dehors, outside.

en avant, forward, in front.
en arrière, back, backwards.
loin, far; **au loin**, in the distance; **lointain** (*adj.*), distant, remote.
ailleurs, elsewhere, somewhere else.
partout, everywhere.

74. SIZE. WEIGHT. SHAPE

grand, large; tall (*of persons*).
important, important; large.
gros, *f.* **grosse**, big, stout; **grossir** (finir), to make bigger, to enlarge.
énorme, enormous, huge; **énormément**, enormously.
immense, immense, vast.
vaste, vast, huge.
petit, small, little; short (*of persons*).
haut, high; **en haut**, at the top; upstairs.
bas, *f.* **basse**, low; **en bas**, at the bottom; downstairs; **il sauta à** (*or* **au**) **bas de son lit**, he jumped out of (down from) his bed.
long, *f.* **longue**, long.
court, short.
large, wide, broad; **la largeur**, width, breadth.
étroit, narrow.
épais, *f.* **épaisse**, thick.
profond, deep; **profondément**, deeply.
léger, light.
lourd, heavy.

Cette pièce a 5 mètres de long *or* **Cette pièce est longue de 5 mètres.** This room is 5 metres long.
Cette pièce a 4 mètres de large *or* **Cette pièce est large de 4 mètres.** This room is 4 metres wide.
Cette tour a 25 mètres de haut *or* **Cette tour est haute de 25 mètres.** This tower is 25 metres high.

le poids, weight; **peser**, to weigh.
le kilogramme *or* **le kilo**, kilogram (= 2·2 lbs.).
la livre (½ kilo), pound (= 1·1 *English lbs.*).
le litre, litre (= 1¾ *pints*).

la forme, form, shape; **former**, to form.
plat, flat.
rond, round.
carré, square.

75. NOUNS RELATING TO ACTION IN GENERAL

une action, action.
le fait, fact ; deed.
un événement, event.
une aventure, adventure ; **un aventurier**, adventurer.
le projet, project, plan, scheme.
le dessein, purpose ; **à dessein**, on purpose.
le but, aim, goal.
le tour, turn ; trick ; **à mon tour**, in my turn ; **à tour de rôle**, in turn ; **faire le tour de**, to go round, *e.g.* nous avons fait le tour des magasins ; **le tour**, little walk, stroll ; **j'ai fait un tour**, I went for a little walk.
la façon, fashion, way.
la manière, manner, way.
la méthode, method.
le motif, motive, reason.
la volonté, will.
la force, might, strength ; **de toutes mes forces**, with all my might.
le besoin, need ; **j'ai besoin de**, I have need of, I need.
le moyen, means, way.
les progrès (*m.*), progress ; **faire des progrès**, to make progress.
une occasion, opportunity, chance.
la chance, luck ; **vous avez de la chance**, you are lucky.
un avantage, advantage.
un inconvénient, inconvenience, disadvantage.
le service, service ; **je vous rends service**, I do you a service, I do you a good turn.
le soin, care ; **soigneux**, careful ; **soigneusement**, carefully ; **il a soin de ses habits**, he takes care of his clothes.
la négligence, negligence, neglect, carelessness ; **négligent**, negligent, careless.
le succès, success.
l' embarras (*m.*), embarrassment, plight, difficulty ; **il me tira d'embarras**, he got me out of my plight (difficulty).
une habitude, habit ; **d'habitude** *or* **d'ordinaire**, usually ; **habituel**, habitual, usual ; **s'habituer à**, to get used to ; **habitué à**, used to.
la coutume, custom ; **comme de coutume**, as usual ; **s'accoutumer à**, to accustom oneself to, to get used to ; **accoutumé à**, accustomed to.

76. ADJECTIVES RELATING TO ACTION

facile, easy ; **facilement**, easily.
simple, simple ; plain ; **simplement**, simply.
difficile, difficult ; **la difficulté**, difficulty ; **sans difficulté**, without difficulty.
possible, possible ; **la possibilité**, possibility ; **impossible**, impossible ; **l'impossibilité** (*f.*), impossibility.
utile, useful ; **inutile**, useless.
pratique, practical ; useful.
commode, convenient ; easy.
puissant, powerful, mighty.
intense, intense.
vif, *f.* **vive**, quick, sharp ; **vivement**, quickly, sharply.
brusque, sudden, abrupt ; **brusquement**, suddenly, abruptly.
adroit, skilful ; **maladroit**, clumsy.
ferme, firm.

77. SOME COMMON TRANSITIVE VERBS

mener, to lead ; **amener**, to bring (*a person*) ; **ramener**, to bring back ; **emmener**, to take (away), *e.g.* je les ai emmenés au cinéma.
conduire (*irr.*), to lead ; to drive ; to conduct ; **se conduire**, to conduct oneself, to behave oneself ; **la conduite**, conduct.
guider, to guide.
accompagner, to accompany.
arrêter, to stop ; to arrest ; il arrêta sa voiture, he stopped his car ; il s'arrêta, he stopped.
croiser, to cross ; to pass (*going in opposite directions*), *e.g.* je l'ai croisé dans la rue, I passed him in the street.
rencontrer, to meet ; **la rencontre**, meeting, encounter ; il alla à leur rencontre, he went to meet them ; il alla au-devant de ses visiteurs, he went to meet his visitors.
suivre (*irr.*), to follow ; to accompany ; **suivant**, following ; **poursuivre**, to pursue, to chase.
envoyer, to send ; **envoyer chercher**, to send for ; **renvoyer**, to send away ; to dismiss.
quitter, to leave.
pousser, to push ; *also* to grow ; **repousser**, to push back (away), to repel, to repulse.
bousculer, to jostle, to push roughly.
heurter, to knock (bump) against, to collide with, *e.g.* il heurta un mur.

renverser, to overturn, to knock down.

traverser, to cross, to go (pass) through.
franchir (finir), to cross, to pass over, *e.g.* ils franchirent une rivière (des collines).
gravir (finir), to climb (=*to walk up anywhere steep*), *e.g.* il gravit la colline.
atteindre (craindre), to attain, to reach, *e.g.* il atteignit le village.

aider, to help, *e.g.* il m'aida à porter les bagages.
servir (dormir), to serve; **servir de**, to serve as, *e.g.* cette pièce sert de cabinet de travail; **servir à** (faire), to serve to (do), *e.g.* cela sert à ouvrir les boîtes; **se servir de**, to make use of, to use, *e.g.* je me sers de cet instrument.
sauver, to save; **se sauver**, to run away.
protéger, to protect.
empêcher, to prevent, *e.g.* je les empêche de sortir.
éviter, to avoid.
surveiller, to watch over, to supervise; **la surveillance**, supervision.
récompenser, to reward; **la récompense**, reward.
offrir (ouvrir), to offer, *e.g.* je lui offris de l'aider.
tendre (vendre), to hold out, to offer, to tender; **(s')étendre**, to spread, to extend, to stretch out.
donner, to give.
rendre (vendre), to render, to give back; **rendre** + *adjective* = to make, *e.g.* ma présence le rend malheureux.
accepter, to accept.
recevoir (*irr.*), to receive.
livrer, to give up.
céder, to yield, to give up.
fournir (finir), to furnish, to supply.

montrer, to show.
indiquer, to indicate, to show.
désigner, to indicate, to point to.
porter, to carry, to bear; to wear; **apporter**, to bring (*a thing*); **rapporter**, to bring back; **emporter**, to carry (take) away; **transporter**, to transport.
mettre (*irr.*), to put; **se mettre à** (faire), to start to (do); **remettre**, to put back; to hand over.
prendre (*irr.*), to take; **reprendre**, to take back; to resume.
poser, to put, to place; je lui pose des questions, I ask him questions; **déposer**, to put down.
disposer, to dispose, to arrange; il dispose d'une grosse fortune, he has a big fortune at his disposal; **se disposer à**, to get ready to.

placer, to place ; **se placer**, to place oneself, to stand.

attraper, to catch ; **rattraper**, to overtake.
ramasser, to pick up.
saisir (finir), to seize.
s' emparer de, to get possession of.
tenir (*irr*), to hold ; **retenir**, to retain, to hold back ; to book (*rooms*, *etc.*) ; **appartenir**, to belong ; **contenir**, to contain ; **maintenir**, to maintain ; **entretenir**, to support, to keep up.
garder, to keep, to guard.
posséder, to possess.
laisser, to let, to allow ; to leave ; **laisser tomber**, to drop.
lâcher, to loose, to let go (of).
se débarrasser de, to get rid of.

cacher, to hide ; **se cacher**, to hide oneself ; **la cachette**, hiding-place.
voler, to steal ; **le vol**, theft.
dérober, to conceal ; to steal ; **se dérober**, to slip away.
chercher, to seek, to look for ; to get ; **envoyer chercher**, to send for ; **à la recherche de**, in search of.
trouver, to find ; **se trouver**, to be found, to be situated ; **retrouver**, to find again, to come across.
examiner, to examine.
lever, to raise ; **se lever**, to get up ; **élever**, to raise, to bring up ; **enlever**, to remove, to take away ; **soulever**, to lift.
dresser, to raise ; to train.

tirer, to pull, to draw ; **attirer**, to attract.
traîner, to drag, to draw ; **entraîner**, to drag away.
écarter, to move aside ; **à l'écart**, aside, out of the way, *e.g.* il restait à l'écart.
entourer, to surround.
border, to border, to line ; **bordé d'arbres**, lined with trees.
envelopper, to envelop ; to wrap up.
plier, to fold.
jeter, to throw ; **se jeter**, to throw oneself.
lancer, to throw, to hurl.
arracher, to snatch, to wrest ; to tear up (*or* out) ; **je lui arrachai le pistolet**, I snatched the pistol from him.
enfoncer, to dig (thrust or drive) in.

briser, to break.
casser, to break, to smash.
rompre (*irr.*), to break (*e.g. chain*, *rope*, *etc.*).
couper, to cut.
déchirer, to tear, to rend.
fendre (vendre), to split, to cleave.
détruire (conduire), to destroy.
démolir (finir), to demolish.
abîmer, to ruin, to damage.

crever, to burst ; to die.
perdre (vendre), to lose ; **la perte**, loss.
égarer, to mislay, to lose ; **s'égarer**, to lose one's way, to stray.

frapper, to strike, to hit.
serrer, to grip, to squeeze ; **il me serra la main**, he shook hands with me.
agiter, to agitate ; to wave.
secouer, to shake.
remuer, to move, to stir ; to wag.
frotter, to rub.
gratter, to scratch.
écraser, to crush.
percer, to pierce.

attacher, to attach, to fasten.
pendre (vendre), to hang ; **pendu au mur**, hanging on the wall.
appuyer, to lean ; to bear on.
ouvrir, to open ; **la porte s'ouvre**, the door opens ; **ouvert**, open, opened ; **entr'ouvert**, half-open, ajar.
couvrir (ouvrir), to cover ; **couvert de**, covered with ; **découvrir**, to discover, to uncover ; **la découverte**, discovery.
fermer, to close, to shut ; **la porte se ferme**, the door closes ; **enfermer**, to shut in ; **renfermer**, to enclose, to contain.
emplir (finir), to fill ; **remplir**, to fill.
répandre (vendre), to spread, to give out, *e.g.* votre cigare répand une bonne odeur.
employer, to employ, to use.
exercer, to exercise.
produire (conduire), to produce.
établir (finir), to establish.
charger, to load ; to entrust, *e.g.* il m'a chargé d'une commission.

choisir (finir), to choose ; **le choix**, choice.
préférer, to prefer, *e.g.* je préfère attendre.
remplacer, to replace.
changer, to change, to alter ; **échanger**, to exchange.
mêler, to mix, to mingle.
mélanger, to mix.
confondre (vendre), to confuse, to mix up.

78. ADJECTIVES DESCRIPTIVE OF CHARACTER AND TEMPERAMENT

bon, *f.* **bonne**, good ; kind ; **à quoi bon attendre?** what is the good of waiting? **la bonté**, goodness, kindness.
gentil, *f.* **gentille**, nice, kind.
doux, *f.* **douce**, sweet ; gentle, mild ; soft ; **doucement**, gently, softly ; **la douceur**, softness, gentleness.
tendre, tender, soft-hearted ;

tendrement, tenderly ; **attendrir** (finir), to affect, to touch, to soften the heart.
indulgent, indulgent, easy-going, soft.
sage, good, well-behaved ; wise.
timide, shy.
sympathique, likeable.
calme, calm, quiet.
tranquille, quiet ; **tranquillement**, quietly ; **la tranquillité**, quietness, peacefulness.
affectueux, affectionate.
dévoué, devoted ; **le dévouement**, devotion.
généreux, generous.
fidèle, faithful.
honnête, honest ; decent.
brave, brave ; good, worthy, honest ; **bravement**, bravely.
juste, just, fair ; **justement**, exactly, precisely ; **juste** (*adv.*), just.
franc, *f.* **franche**, frank, candid ; **franchement**, frankly.
patient, patient ; **impatient**, impatient ; **la patience**, patience ; **perdre patience**, to lose patience.
prudent, prudent, careful ; **imprudent**, imprudent, unwise ; **la prudence**, prudence.
sérieux, serious, earnest ; **sérieusement**, seriously, earnestly.
sévère, severe, stern ; **sévèrement**, severely, sternly.
digne, worthy, dignified.
fier, (justifiably) proud ; **fièrement**, proudly.
naturel, *f.* **naturelle**, natural ; **naturellement**, naturally, of course.
convenable, suitable ; decent, respectable.
de bonne humeur, in a good humour, good-tempered ; **de mauvaise humeur**, in a bad humour, bad-tempered.

79. NOUNS AND ADJECTIVES RELATING TO MIND AND THOUGHT

l' esprit (*m.*), mind ; spirit ; wit.
le sens, sense ; **sensé**, sensible.
la raison, reason ; **j'ai raison**, I am right ; **j'ai tort**, I am wrong ; **raisonnable**, reasonable.
une idée, idea.
une intention, intention ; **j'ai l'intention de rester**, I intend to stay.
un avis, warning ; opinion ; **à mon avis**, in my opinion.

intelligent, intelligent, clever.
habile, able, clever.
rusé, crafty.

malin, *f.* **maligne**, sly, cunning.
sûr, sure ; **sûrement**, surely.
certain, certain ; **certainement**, certainly.
probable, probable, likely ; **probablement**, probably.
vrai, true ; **vraiment**, **truly**, really ; **la vérité**, truth.
évident, evident, obvious ; **évidemment**, evidently, obviously.
véritable, veritable, **real.**
secret, *f.* **secrète**, **secret.**

80. VERBS RELATING TO THOUGHT AND UNDERSTANDING

croire (*irr.*), to believe, to think ; **incroyable**, incredible.
penser, to think ; **je pense bien !** I should think so! **la pensée**, thought.
réfléchir (finir), to reflect, to think, to ponder, *e.g.* je réfléchissais à mon travail.
songer, to dream ; to think, *e.g.* il songeait à son malheur.
rêver, to dream ; **le rêve**, dream.
savoir (*irr.*), to know.
ignorer, to ignore ; not to know, *e.g.* j'ignore ses raisons.
remarquer, to notice ; **remarquable**, remarkable.
comprendre (prendre), to understand ; **y compris le vin**, including (the) wine.
se rendre compte de, to realize, *e.g.* il se rendit compte de sa situation.
concevoir (recevoir), to conceive.
deviner, to guess, to surmise.
supposer, to suppose.
considérer, to consider ; **to stare at.**
s' imaginer, to imagine.
se figurer, to imagine.
sembler, to seem ; **il me semble que**, it seems to me that.
hésiter, to hesitate, *e.g.* j'hésite à le croire.
se souvenir (venir), to remember, *e.g.* je me souviens de cet incident ; **le souvenir**, memory, recollection.
se rappeler, to remember, *e.g.* je me rappelle ses paroles.
oublier, to forget, *e.g.* j'ai oublié de fermer la porte.
mériter, to deserve, *e.g.* vous méritez de réussir.
se fier à, to trust (to), *e.g.* je ne me fie pas à ses promesses.
convenir (venir), to agree, *e.g.* ils sont convenus de se séparer ; **convenir**, to suit, *e.g.* cette heure ne leur convient pas.

être d'accord, to agree, to be in agreement.
conclure (*irr.*), to conclude.
intéresser, to interest; **s'intéresser à**, to interest oneself in, *e.g.* il s'intéresse à la littérature; **intéressant**, interesting.
signifier, to signify, to mean.
prouver, to prove; **la preuve**, proof.
inventer, to invent.
convaincre (**vaincre**), to convince.

81. VERBS RELATING TO COMPULSION AND EFFORT

faire (*irr.*), to do, to make; **qu'allez-vous faire de cet argent?** what are you going to do with this money?
pouvoir (*irr.*), to be able, *e.g.* il ne peut pas marcher.
devoir (+*infin.*), to have to, *e.g.* **je dois rentrer**, I must go home.
falloir; **il faut**, it is necessary, *e.g.* **il me faut partir**, I must go.
agir (finir), to act; **il s'agit de**, it is a question (matter) of.
obliger, to oblige; to compel; **obligé**, obliged, *e.g.* vous êtes obligé de payer.
forcer, to force; **s'efforcer** (de), to try hard (to), *e.g.* il s'efforça de courir.
contraindre (craindre), to constrain, to compel.
oser, to dare, *e.g.* j'ose parler.
essayer, to try, *e.g.* il essaya de courir.
décider, to decide, *e.g.* je décide de rester; **se décider** (à), to make up one's mind (to), *e.g.* il se décida à rester.
résoudre (*irr.*), to resolve.
réussir (finir), to succeed, *e.g.* il réussit à sortir.
infliger, to inflict.
profiter de, to profit by, to take advantage of, *e.g.* il profita de mes conseils.
prendre garde, to take care, to be careful.
avoir beau (faire), to (do) in vain, *e.g.* **vous avez beau essayer**, you may try in vain, it is no use your trying.
être en train de (faire), to be in the act of (doing), *e.g.* **je suis en train d'écrire quelques lettres**, I am just writing a few letters.
j'ai failli tomber, I nearly fell; **il faillit** (*p. hist.*) **tomber**, he nearly fell.

82. ADJECTIVES RELATING TO PLEASURE

heureux, happy, *e.g.* je suis heureux de vous voir ; **heureusement**, happily, fortunately; **le bonheur**, happiness, good fortune ; **par bonheur**, by good fortune, luckily ; **malheureux**, unhappy ; **malheureusement**, unhappily, unfortunately ; **le malheur**, unhappiness, misfortune.

content, glad, pleased, *e.g.* nous sommes contents de le savoir ; **mécontent**, displeased, dissatisfied ; **se contenter**, to content oneself, to be satisfied, *e.g.* il se contenta de protester.

gai, gay, jolly ; **gaiement**, gaily ; **la gaieté**, gaiety ; **égayer**, to cheer up, to brighten.

joyeux, joyful, joyous, merry ; **joyeusement**, joyfully ; **la joie**, joy.

agréable, agreeable, pleasant ; **désagréable**, disagreeable, unpleasant.

charmant, charming.

exquis, exquisite.

délicieux, delicious, delightful.

enchanté, delighted, *e.g.* je suis enchanté de faire votre connaissance.

à l'aise, at one's ease, comfortable ; **à mon aise**, at my ease, comfortable.

magnifique, magnificent.

superbe, superb, lovely.

admirable, admirable, lovely.

excellent, excellent.

parfait, perfect.

célèbre, celebrated, famous.

fameux, famous ; wonderful.

83. WORDS RELATING TO WISHING AND FEELING

vouloir (*irr.*), to wish, to want ; **je veux dire . . .** I mean . . . ; **je leur en veux**, I bear them a grudge.

désirer, to desire, *e.g.* je désire les voir.

souhaiter, to wish (=*to express a wish*), *e.g.* je lui souhaitai le bonjour.

plaire (*irr.*), to please ; **il plaît à mes parents**, he pleases my parents, *or* my parents like him ; **déplaire**, to displease.

espérer, to hope ; **l'espoir** (*m.*), hope (*in the general sense*) ; **l'espérance** (*f.*), hope (=*a specific hope*), *e.g.* il trompa mes espérances.

jouir (finir), to enjoy, *e.g.* nous jouissons de notre

liberté ; **réjouir**, to rejoice, to gladden, *e.g.* le soleil les réjouit.

ravir (finir), to delight.

satisfaire (faire), to satisfy ; **satisfait**, satisfied.

sentir (dormir), to feel ; to smell ; **ressentir**, to feel (*an emotion or sensation*), *e.g.* je ressentis une vive émotion ; **le sentiment**, feeling ; **réprimer un sentiment**, to repress a feeling.

éprouver, to feel, to experience.

une envie, wish, desire, inclination ; **j'ai envie de me reposer**, I want to rest, I feel like resting.

Je vous sais gré de votre bonne action. I am grateful to you for your kind action.

84. SURPRISE AND FEAR

étonner, to astonish, to surprise ; **s'étonner**, to be surprised ; **étonnant**, surprising ; **l'étonnement** (*m.*), astonishment, surprise.

surprendre (prendre), to surprise ; to overhear ; **je leur fais une surprise**, I give them a surprise.

ému, moved, thrilled ; **émouvant**, exciting, thrilling.

la merveille, marvel ; **merveilleux**, marvellous.

drôle, funny.

étrange, strange.

singulier, singular, strange.

curieux, curious ; inquisitive.

ridicule, ridiculous.

effrayer, to frighten, to scare ; **effrayant**, frightening ; **la frayeur**, fright.

épouvanter, to terrify, to scare ; **épouvantable**, awful, terrifying.

bouleverser, to upset.

redouter, to dread.

inspirer, to inspire.

la peur, fear ; **j'ai peur de le déranger**, I am afraid to disturb him, I am afraid of disturbing him ; **vous lui faites peur**, you frighten him ; **de peur de tomber**, for fear of falling.

craindre (*irr.*), to fear, *e.g.* je craignais de les rencontrer ; **la crainte**, fear.

l' effroi (*m.*), dread ; **effroyable**, dreadful.

stupéfait, bewildered, taken aback.

effaré, startled.

affreux, frightful.

formidable, formidable, terrific.

85. FEELINGS OF DEPRESSION

triste, sad; **tristement**, sadly; **la tristesse**, sadness.
morne, gloomy.
grave, grave, serious.
le **chagrin**, sorrow.
l' **angoisse** (*f.*), anguish, distress.
la **peine**, trouble; **à peine**, hardly, scarcely; **ce n'est pas la peine** *or* **cela n'en vaut pas la peine**, it is not worth while; **pénible**, hard, distressing.
le **souci**, care, worry, trouble; **soucieux**, anxious, worried, careworn; **se soucier** (de), to care *or* worry (about).
le **désespoir**, despair.
la **pitié**, pity; **avoir pitié de**, to take pity on.
la **déception**, disappointment; **décevoir** (recevoir), to disappoint; **déçu**, disappointed.
le **soupçon**, suspicion; **soupçonner**, to suspect; **soupçonneux**, suspicious (=*harbouring suspicion*).
la **honte**, shame; **j'ai honte de cette action**, I am ashamed of that action; **honteux**, ashamed, shameful.

regretter, to regret, to be sorry, *e.g.* je regrette de refuser.
inquiéter, to disturb, to make anxious; **s'inquiéter**, to be worried, to worry; **inquiet**, anxious, worried; **l'inquiétude** (*f.*), anxiety, disquiet.
tourmenter, to torment; **se tourmenter**, to worry.
plaindre (craindre), to pity; **se plaindre**, to complain.
ennuyer, to bore, to weary; **s'ennuyer**, to be bored; **ennuyeux**, boring, tiresome.
fatiguer, to tire; **se fatiguer**, to get tired; **fatigué**, tired; **fatigant**, tiring; **las**, *f.* **lasse**, weary.
épuiser, to exhaust; **épuisé**, exhausted.
accabler, to overwhelm, to wear down; **accablé de fatigue**, overcome with fatigue.
supporter, to support; to endure, to bear; **insupportable**, unbearable.
subir (finir), to undergo.
étouffer, to stifle.
gêner, to embarrass, to trouble.
déranger, to trouble.
agacer, to irritate.
gronder, to scold, reprove, grumble at.
taquiner, to tease.
se moquer de, to make fun of.

86. WEAKNESS AND DECEIT

faible, weak ; **la faiblesse**, weakness.
stupide, stupid.
bête, stupid, silly.
paresseux, lazy.
naïf, *f.* **naïve**, ingenuous, simple.
distrait, absent-minded, thoughtless.
confus, confused.
fou, *f.* **folle**, mad, wild ; **follement**, madly, wildly ; **la folie**, madness, folly.

le défaut, fault, failing.
la sottise, foolishness, silly act.
tromper, to deceive ; **se tromper**, to be mistaken.
mentir (dormir), to lie ; **le mensonge**, lie.
tenter, to tempt ; to attempt, *e.g.* il tenta de les sauver ; **la tentation**, temptation.
faire semblant de, to pretend, *e.g.* il faisait semblant de dormir.
feindre (craindre), to feign, to pretend, *e.g.* il feignit de me croire.
abuser de, to take (unfair) advantage of, *e.g.* vous abusez de ma patience.
tricher, to cheat.
gâter, to spoil ; **gâté**, spoilt.

87. BAD FEELINGS

la colère, anger, rage ; **se mettre en colère**, to get angry, to lose one's temper.
la haine, hatred ; **haïr** (*irr.*), to hate.
le mépris, contempt, scorn ; **mépriser**, to contemn, to despise, to scorn.
le dédain, disdain ; **dédaigner**, to disdain.
l' orgueil (*m.*), (*arrogant*) pride ; **orgueilleux**, proud, conceited.
une injure, insult.
la menace, threat ; **menacer**, to threaten, *e.g.* il menaça de me frapper.
la dispute, quarrel ; **se disputer**, to quarrel.
la querelle, quarrel ; **se quereller**, to quarrel.
la punition, punishment , **punir** (finir), to punish.
le châtiment, punishment.

fâcher, to vex, to anger ; **se fâcher**, to get angry ; **fâché**, vexed, upset, angry.
se vanter, to boast.
venger, to avenge ; **se**

venger, to avenge oneself, to take one's revenge ; **la vengeance**, vengeance, revenge.

trahir (finir), to betray.

nuire (*irr.*), to harm, to damage, *e.g.* cela nuit à nos intérêts.

mauvais, bad ; wicked ; **mal**, badly.

méchant, wicked ; **méchamment**, wickedly ; **la méchanceté**, wickedness.

vilain, ugly, nasty.

suspect, suspect, suspicious (=*under suspicion*).

méfiant, distrustful, suspicious.

coupable, guilty.

faux, *f.* **fausse**, false.

cruel, *f.* **cruelle**, cruel.

odieux, odious.

furieux, furious.

féroce, ferocious, savage.

violent, violent ; **violemment**, violently.

rude, hard, rough.

88. CONJUNCTIONS

mais, but.

eh bien, well (*when one is beginning to speak*), *e.g.* Eh bien, mon ami, comment allez-vous?

donc, therefore ; so, then (=*therefore*).

ou, or ; **ou bien**, or else.

peut-être, perhaps.

car, for.

quand, when.

lorsque, when (*but not in questions*).

comme, as ; **comme si**, as if, as though.

comment, how.

pendant que, while (=*during the time that*).

tandis que, whilst (*with an idea of contrast*), *e.g.* André est resté à Paris, tandis que son frere est allé à Londres.

au moment où, at the moment when, just as.

dès que, as soon as.

aussitôt que, as soon as.

pourquoi, why.

parce que, because.

puisque, since, seeing that, *e.g.* je ne vous le dirai pas, puisque vous le savez déjà.

aussi bien que, as well as.

cependant, however.

pourtant, however, yet ; **et pourtant il est riche, and yet he is rich.**

sans doute, doubtless, very likely.

en effet, indeed.

d'ailleurs, besides, moreover.

bien entendu, of course.

par conséquent, consequently.

néanmoins, nevertheless.

89. PREPOSITIONS

dans, in, into.
devant, in front of, before (*position*).
avant, before (*time or order*), *e.g.* avant six heures; il est arrivé avant moi.
après, after; **d'après**, according to.
derrière, behind.
sur, on.
sous, under.
au-dessus de, above; over.
au-dessous de, below.
par-dessus, over, *e.g.* il lança un caillou par-dessus le mur.
avec, with.
sans, without.
pour, for.
contre, against.
entre, between.
parmi, among.
au milieu de, in the middle of.
au centre de, in the centre of.
en haut de, at the top of.
en bas de, at the bottom of.
au fond de, at the bottom of; **du fond de**, from the bottom (the depths) of; **à fond**, thoroughly, *e.g.* il connaît ce sujet à fond.
près de, near (to); **tout près de**, quite near to, just by; **de près**, closely, *e.g.* je le regardai de près.
à côté de, beside, next to.
au bord de, by the side of, on the bank of.
le long de, along.
autour de, round.
en face de, opposite.
par, by, through.
vers, towards; **envers**, towards (*of behaviour*), *e.g.* respectueux envers nos maîtres.
à travers, across, through; **à travers champs**, across country
jusqu'à, as far as, up to, until.
au delà de, beyond.
hors de, out of.
pendant, during, for.
depuis, since.
au bout de, at the end of; after, *e.g.* au bout d'un mois.
malgré, in spite of.
sauf, except, save.
excepté, except.
à cause de, because of.
grâce à, thanks to.
au lieu de, instead of.
au sujet de, about, *e.g.* nous parlions au sujet de son fils.
selon, according to.

90. SOME ADVERBS OF MANNER

très, very.
fort, very.
presque, almost, nearly.
surtout, above all, especially.
aussi, also, too; so.
bien, well; **mieux**, better; **je fais de mon mieux**, I do my best; **vous feriez mieux de**

rester ici, you had better stay here.
mal, badly.
tout à fait, quite.
juste, just, exactly.
environ, about, approximately.
ainsi, thus.
en vain, in vain.
généralement, generally; **en général**, generally, in general.
exprès, on purpose.
volontiers, gladly, willingly.
au hasard, at random; **par hasard**, by chance.
tellement, so, *e.g.* **je suis tellement fatigué.**
absolument, absolutely.
infiniment, infinitely.
extrêmement, extremely.

PART II

ENGLISH–FRENCH VOCABULARY

(in alphabetical order)

NOTE

All verbs marked as irregular (*irr.*) are shown in the Verb List. All verbs shown in brackets as types to be consulted, are in the Verb List, *e.g. craindre, tenir*, as in *peindre* (*craindre*), *contenir* (*tenir*).

In some instances, alternatives are given in brackets, both in French and English. Thus " to take (bring) up " means of course " to take up " or " to bring up ". " To get ready to (do)," *se préparer* (*se disposer, s'apprêter*) *à* (*faire*) means that one can say the same thing in three ways : *se préparer à* (*faire*), *se disposer à* (*faire*), *s'apprêter à* (*faire*).

The examples provided should be carefully noted, especially those showing the construction taken by verbs. Thus, under " to tell " we give the example : *je lui dis d'attendre*, to remind you that " to tell someone to do something " is, in French, *dire à quelqu'un de faire quelque chose.* The examples will help you to say correctly what you want to say.

ABBREVIATIONS USED

adj., adjective
adv., adverb
conj., conjunction
fam., familiar
fut., future
invar., invariable
irr., irregular
p. hist., past historic
pl., plural
prep., preposition
subj., subjunctive
trans., transitive
intrans., intransitive

A

able (*adj.*), habile.

able ; to be able, pouvoir (*irr.*).

about (=*round*), autour de ; (=*approximately*) environ, *e.g.* à 4 heures environ ; vers, *e.g.* vers 7 heures ; à peu près, *e.g.* à peu près 15 kilomètres ; (=*concerning*), au sujet de, à propos de ; **to be about to** (do), être sur le point de (faire) *or* aller (faire), *e.g.* j'étais sur le point de sortir, *or* j'allais sortir ; **what are you talking about?** de quoi parlez-vous? **what is it (all) about?** de quoi s'agit-il? **to turn about,** faire demi-tour.

above, au-dessus de ; **above all,** surtout.

abroad, à l'étranger.

abrupt (*slope, etc.*), abrupt ; (*action, speech*) brusque ;

abruptly (*action*), brusquement.

absence, l'absence (*f.*) ; **in the absence of,** en l'absence de.

absent-minded, distrait.

absolutely, absolument.

abyss, un abîme.

accent, un accent.

to **accept,** accepter.

accident, un accident.

to **accompany,** accompagner ; suivre (*irr.*).

according to, selon, d'après, suivant.

accordingly, donc.
account (=*story*), le récit.
to accustom oneself to, s'accoutumer à.
ache, le mal ; **I have a headache**, j'ai mal à la tête ; **I have tooth-ache**, j'ai mal aux dents.
to acknowledge (=*give a greeting*), saluer ; (*error, act*) reconnaître.
acquaintance, la connaissance.
to acquire, acquérir (*irr.*).
across, à travers ; **across country**, à travers champs ; **to come across** (*person or thing*), retrouver.
to act, agir (finir).
action, un acte, une action.
active, actif, *f.* active.
actor, un acteur ; **actress**, une actrice.
to add, ajouter.
address, une adresse.
to address oneself to, s'adresser à.
adjoining, voisin, contigu.
admirable, admirable.
to admire, admirer.
to admit, admettre (mettre).
to adore, adorer.
to advance, (s') avancer.
advantage, un avantage ; **to take advantage of**, profiter de, *e.g.* nous avons profité du beau temps.
adventure, une aventure ; **adventurer**, un aventurier.
advice, des conseils (*m.*) ; **a piece of advice**, un conseil.
to advise, conseiller, *e.g.* je lui conseille de rester.
aeroplane, un aéroplane, un avion ; **by plane**, en avion.
to affect (*one's feelings*), attendrir (finir), toucher.
affectionate, affectueux ; **affectionately**, affectueusement.
to afford ; I cannot afford to buy it, je n'ai pas les moyens de l'acheter.
afraid ; to be afraid, avoir peur, *e.g.* j'ai peur de sortir ; **I am very afraid**, j'ai grand'peur.
afresh, de nouveau.
Africa, l'Afrique (*f.*) ; **South Africa**, l'Afrique du Sud ; **South African**, le Sud-Africain ; **African**, africain.
after, après ; (=*at the end of*), au bout de, *e.g.* au bout de quelques minutes, il revint ; **after(wards)** (*adv.*), après, ensuite ; **the day after**, le lendemain ; **after seeing**, après avoir vu ; **to come after**, suivre (*irr.*), succéder à.
afternoon, un après-midi, *pl.* des après-midi ; **good afternoon** (*on meeting*), bonjour.
again, encore, de nouveau.
against, contre.
age, l'âge (*m.*) ; (=*century, period*) le siècle ; **what is your age?** quel âge avez-vous? **old age**, la vieillesse ; **to age**, vieillir (finir).
to agitate, agiter ; **agitated**, agité.
ago, il y a, *e.g.* **a month ago**, il y a un mois.
to agree, s'entendre (vendre), *e.g.* nous nous entendons bien ; **to agree to** (do), convenir de (faire), *e.g.* ils sont convenus de se séparer ; **to be in agreement**, être d'accord.
agreeable, agréable.
aim, le but.
air, l'air (*m.*) ; **in(to) the air**, en l'air ; **by air**, en avion.
airport, un aéroport.
ajar, entr'ouvert.
alarmed, effrayé, alarmé.

alas! hélas!

alike, semblable, pareil, *f.* pareille.

alive, vivant, en vie.

all, tout, etc. ; **not at all,** pas du tout ; **all right!** très (fort) bien! soit!

alley-way, la ruelle.

to **allow,** permettre (mettre), *e.g.* je lui permets d'entrer ; laisser, *e.g.* je le laisse entrer.

almost, presque.

alone, seul ; **all alone,** tout seul.

along, le long de, *e.g.* il courait le long de la haie ; **I was walking along the street,** je marchais dans la rue ; **I was walking along the road,** je marchais sur la route ; **to go along (by),** longer, *e.g.* je longeais la rivière ; **to go (travel) along** (*of vehicles*), marcher, rouler.

aloud, à haute voix.

already, déjà.

also, aussi.

to **alter,** changer.

although, quoique, bien que (+*subj.*).

altogether (=*wholly*), tout à fait.

always, toujours.

America, l'Amérique (*f.*) ; **American,** un Américain, *f.* une Américaine.

among, parmi ; **they were talking among themselves,** ils parlaient entre eux.

to **amuse,** amuser ; **to amuse oneself,** s'amuser ; **amusing,** amusant ; **amusement,** un amusement, le divertissement, la distraction.

ancient, ancien, *f.* ancienne, *e.g.* une maison ancienne.

anger, la colère ; **to anger,** fâcher, mettre en colère ; **angry,** fâché, en colère ; **to get angry,** se fâcher, se mettre en colère.

anguish, l'angoisse (*f.*).

animal, un animal (*pl.* -aux) ; la bête.

to **announce,** annoncer.

to **annoy,** vexer, fâcher, ennuyer ; **annoying,** ennuyeux.

answer, la réponse ; **to answer,** répondre (vendre), *e.g.* je réponds à sa question ; **to answer for,** répondre de.

ant, la fourmi.

anxiety, l'inquiétude (*f.*), l'anxiété (*f.*).

anxious, anxieux, inquiet ; (=*careworn*) soucieux ; **to make anxious,** inquiéter, *e.g.* cette nouvelle nous inquiéta ; **to be anxious to (do),** tenir à (faire).

any ; **have you any money?** avez-vous de l'argent? **I haven't any,** je n'en ai pas ; **without any difficulty,** sans aucune difficulté ; **in any town,** dans n'importe quelle ville ; **bring a book—any one,** apportez un livre, n'importe lequel.

anybody ; **I do not meet anybody,** je ne rencontre personne ; **without meeting anybody,** sans rencontrer personne ; **anybody will tell you,** n'importe qui vous le dira.

anything, quelque chose, *e.g.* vous a-t-il donné quelque chose? **not anything,** ne ... rien, *e.g.* il n'a rien dit ; **without saying anything,** sans rien dire ; **do you need anything else?** avez-vous besoin d'autre chose? **sing anything,** chantez n'importe quoi.

anywhere ; he goes anywhere, il va n'importe où ; **have you seen him anywhere?** l'avez-vous vu quelque part? **I have not seen him anywhere,** je ne l'ai vu nulle part.

apartment, un appartement.

to apologize, faire des excuses ; s'excuser (de) ; **apology,** une excuse.

appeal, un appel.

to appear, paraître (connaître), apparaître ; **it appears that,** il paraît que.

appetite, l'appétit (*m.*).

to applaud, applaudir (finir).

apple, la pomme ; **apple-tree,** le pommier.

to apply to, s'adresser à.

to appoint (*a person*), nommer, *e.g.* il a été nommé directeur.

to approach (=*draw near a place*), approcher de, *e.g.* nous approchons de la ville ; *otherwise* s'approcher de.

approximately, environ, à peu près.

apricot, un abricot.

April, avril (*m.*) ; **in April,** en avril, au mois d'avril.

apron, le tablier.

to argue, discuter ; **argument,** un argument, une discussion.

arm, le bras ; (*weapon*) une arme.

armchair, le fauteuil.

around (*prep.*), autour de.

to arrange, disposer.

to arrest, arrêter.

to arrive, arriver (*with* être) ; **arrival,** une arrivée ; **on my arrival,** à mon arrivée.

arrow, la flèche.

article, un article.

as (*starting a sentence*), **comme** ; (=*in proportion as, as gradually*) à mesure que, *e.g.* à mesure que nous approchons de la ville ; **as if (though),** comme si, *e.g.* comme s'il ne comprenait pas ; **as if (though) to,** comme pour ; **as soon as,** dès que, aussitôt que ; **as far as,** jusqu'à ; **as for (you),** quant à (vous) ; **as much (many),** autant.

ascent, l'ascension (*f.*).

ash, la cendre ; **ash-tray,** le cendrier.

ashamed, honteux ; **to be ashamed,** avoir honte, *e.g.* j'ai honte de cette action.

ashore, à terre.

aside, à l'écart ; **to move aside,** (s') écarter ; **to put aside,** mettre de côté.

to ask, demander, *e.g.* je lui demande un crayon ; je lui demande de venir ; **to ask** (*polite request*), prier, *e.g.* je le prie d'entrer ; **to ask oneself,** se demander ; **to ask a question,** poser une question ; **to ask about (after),** s'informer de.

asleep, endormi ; **to be asleep,** dormir (*irr.*), **to fall asleep,** s'endormir.

to assemble, (s') assembler, (se) rassembler.

to assist, assister, secourir (courir) ; **assistance,** le secours.

to assume, supposer.

Assumption, feast of the, (August 15), l'Assomption (*f.*).

to assure, assurer, **to assure oneself,** s'assurer.

to astonish, étonner ; **to be aston-**

ished, s'étonner ; **astonishment**, l'étonnement (*m.*).

at, à ; **at first**, d'abord ; **at last**, enfin ; **at once**, tout de suite, immédiatement, aussitôt.

to attach, attacher.

attack, une attaque ; **to attack**, attaquer.

to attain, atteindre (craindre).

to attempt, tenter, *e.g.* il tenta de s'évader.

to attend (*medically*), soigner, *e.g.* le médecin soigne ses malades ; (=*pay attention*) faire attention.

attention, l'attention. (*f.*) ; **to pay attention**, faire attention.

attentively, attentivement.

attic, la mansarde.

to attract, attirer ; **attractive**, attirant, attrayant.

August, août (*m.*) ; **in August**, en août, au mois d'août.

aunt, la tante ; **auntie**, ma tante.

Australia, l'Australie (*f.*) ; **Australian**, un Australien (*f.* -ienne) ; (*adj.*) australien.

author, un auteur.

autumn, l'automne (*m.*) ; **in autumn**, en automne, à l'automne ; **an autumn day**, un jour d'automne.

to avenge, venger ; **to avenge oneself**, se venger.

average, la moyenne ; **on an (the) average**, en moyenne.

to avoid, éviter, *e.g.* il évitait de les rencontrer.

avowal, un aveu.

to await, attendre (vendre).

to awake, s'éveiller, se réveiller.

away ; **far away**, au loin ; **some distance away**, à quelque distance ; **to go away**, s'en aller ; **to walk (move) away**, s'éloigner ; **to run away**, se sauver, s'enfuir (fuir) ; **to slip away**, se dérober, s'esquiver ; **to carry away**, emporter ; **to take away**, emporter, enlever ; **to lead away**, emmener ; **to drag away**, entraîner ; **to send away**, renvoyer ; **to push away**, repousser ; **to look away**, détourner les yeux (la tête).

awful, affreux, épouvantable.

axe, la hache.

B

baby, le bébé.

bachelor, le célibataire.

back (*noun*), le dos ; (*of a chair*) le dossier ; **at the back of the room**, au fond de la salle ; **at the back**, par derrière ; **back (wards)** (*direction*), en arrière ; **to be back**, être de retour ; **to come back**, revenir (*with* être) ; **to go back**, retourner (*with* être) ; **to give back** rendre (vendre) ; **to put back**, remettre ; **to hold back**, retenir ; **to push back**, repousser ; **to move back**, reculer.

bacon, le bacon, le lard.

bad, mauvais ; **badly**, mal.

bag, le sac ; **handbag**, le sac à main.

baker, le boulanger ; **baker's shop**, **bakery**, la boulangerie.

ball (=*dance*), le bal.

ball (*tennis, golf, etc*), la balle ; (*football*) le ballon ; (=*something round*) la boule, *e.g.* une boule de neige (de papier).

balloon, le ballon.

banana, la banane.

bank (*money*), la banque.

bank (*river, etc.*), la rive, le bord ; **on the bank of**, au bord de.

bare, nu.

barely, à peine.

to **bark**, aboyer; **bark, barking**, l'aboiement (*m.*).

barn, la grange.

barracks, la caserne.

barrel (*container*), le tonneau; (*of a gun*) le canon.

barrister, un avocat.

basin, le bol.

basket (*with handle*), le panier; (*without top handle, e.g. for linen, waste paper*) la corbeille.

bath, le bain, **bathroom**, la salle de bains; **bathe**, le bain; **to bathe**, se baigner; **bather**, le baigneur (*f.* -euse).

battle, la bataille; **to give battle**, livrer bataille.

bay, la baie.

beach, la plage.

beak, le bec.

bean (broad), la fève; **kidney bean, haricot bean**, le haricot; **French bean**, le haricot vert.

bear, un ours.

to **bear** (=*carry*) porter; (= *endure*) supporter.

beard, la barbe.

beast, la bête.

to **beat**, battre (*irr.*).

beat (*policeman's, etc.*), la tournée.

beautiful, beau (bel *before vowel*), *f.* belle; **beautifully**, admirablement; **beauty**, la beauté.

because, parce que; **because of**, à cause de.

to **beckon**, faire signe à, *e.g.* je leur fais signe.

to **become**, devenir (*with* être); **what has become of him?** qu'est-il devenu?

bed, le lit; **to go to bed**, se coucher; **in bed**, couché, au lit; **bedroom**, la chambre (à coucher); **bed-side book**, le livre de chevet.

bee, une abeille.

beech (**-tree**), le hêtre.

beefsteak, le bifteck.

beer, la bière.

before (*position*), devant; (*time or order*) avant, *e.g.* il arriva avant moi, avant midi, **the day (evening) before**, la veille; **a few months before**, quelques mois auparavant; **before time**, en avance; **I have been here before**, je suis déjà venu ici; **before (doing)**, avant de (faire); **before** (*conj.*), avant que +*subj.*

to **beg** (=*ask for charity*), mendier; **beggar**, le mendiant.

to **beg** (= *ask politely*), prier, *e.g.* je vous prie de m'excuser.

to **begin**, commencer; **to begin to** (do), commencer à (faire), se mettre à (faire), *e.g.* ils commencent à jouer, ils se mettent à jouer.

beginning, le commencement.

to **behave**, se conduire, se comporter; **well-behaved**, sage; **behaviour**, la conduite.

behind, derrière.

being; **human being**, un être humain.

Belgium, la Belgique; **Belgian**, le (la) Belge; (*adj.*) belge.

to **believe**, croire (*irr.*); **to believe in**, croire à, *e.g.* je ne crois pas aux miracles.

bell (*church, etc.*), la cloche; (*house*) la sonnette.

to **bellow** (*cattle*), beugler, mugir (finir).

to **belong**, appartenir (tenir);

(=*be a member of*) faire partie de, *e.g.* il fait partie de notre club.

below (*prep.*), au-dessous de ; (*adv.*) en bas.

belt, la ceinture.

to bend (over), se pencher ; **to bend** (=*stoop down*), se baisser.

beside, à côté de, auprès de.

besides, d'ailleurs.

best (*adj.*), le meilleur ; (*adv.*) le mieux ; **to do one's best**, faire de son mieux.

to betray, trahir (finir).

better (*adj.*), meilleur, *e.g.* un meilleur livre ; (*adv.*) mieux, *e.g.* vous jouez mieux ; **he is better** (*in health*), il va mieux ; **it is better to (do)**, il vaut mieux (faire) ; **you had better stay here**, vous feriez mieux de rester ici.

between, entre.

bewildered, stupéfait.

beyond, au delà de ; (*adv.*) plus loin ; **to go beyond**, dépasser.

bicycle, la bicyclette ; **to ride a bicycle**, monter à bicyclette ; **to travel (go along) on a bicycle**, rouler à bicyclette.

big, grand ; (=*bulky, stout*) gros, *f.* grosse.

bike, le vélo.

bill (*hotel*), la note ; (*restaurant, café*) l'addition (*f.*).

bird, un oiseau.

biro, le bic.

birth, la naissance ; **birthday**, l'anniversaire (*m.*), la fête ; **birth-place**, le lieu de naissance ; (*of a movement, etc.*) le berceau.

bit, le morceau.

to bite, mordre (vendre).

black, noir ; **to blacken**, noircir (finir).

blackberry, la mûre sauvage.

blackboard, le tableau noir.

blanket, la couverture.

to bleed, saigner ; **bleeding**, saignant, en sang.

to bless, bénir (finir) ; **God bless you**, Dieu vous bénisse

blind, aveugle ; **blindly**, aveuglément.

blood, le sang.

blot, la tache (d'encre).

blotting-paper, le (papier) buvard.

blouse, la blouse.

blow, le coup ; **they come to blows**, ils en viennent aux mains.

to blow, souffler ; **to blow one's nose**, se moucher.

blue, bleu, *pl.* bleus.

to blush, rougir (finir).

board (*wood*), la planche ; (=*notice-board*) un écriteau ; (*meals*) la pension ; **to board**, prendre pension ; **boarding-house**, la pension ; **boarder**, le (la) pensionnaire.

to boast (of, about), se vanter (de).

boat, le bateau ; **fishing-boat**, la barque de pêche ; **rowing-boat**, le canot, une embarcation.

body, le corps ; **dead body**, le cadavre.

boiling, bouillant.

bold, hardi ; **boldly**, hardiment ; **boldness**, la hardiesse.

bolt (*locking*), le verrou.

bone, un os.

book, le livre ; **second-hand book**, un livre d'occasion ; **exercise book**, le cahier ; **note-book**, le carnet ; **book-case**, la bibliothèque ; **book-seller,** le libraire ; **bookshop,** la librairie.

to **book** (*room, seat, etc.*), retenir (tenir).

boot, le soulier.

to **border,** border ; **bordered with,** bordé de.

to **bore,** ennuyer ; **to be bored,** s'ennuyer ; **boring,** ennuyeux.

born, né ; **to be born,** naître (*irr.*) ; **he was born,** il est né *or* il naquit.

to **borrow,** emprunter, *e.g.* il emprunta de l'argent à son frère.

boss, le patron.

both, tous (les) deux, *f.* toutes (les) deux ; **he was both stupid and lazy,** il était à la fois stupide et paresseux.

to **bother,** déranger.

bottle, la bouteille.

bottom, le fond ; **at the bottom of the sea,** au fond de la mer ; **from the bottom of,** du fond de ; **at the bottom of the hill,** au bas de la colline.

boulevard, le boulevard.

to **bound,** bondir (finir).

to **bow,** s'incliner ; (=*polite greeting*) saluer.

bowl, le bol, une écuelle.

box, la boîte.

boy, le garçon ; (*in school*) un élève.

bracelet, le bracelet.

brake, le frein ; **to brake,** freiner, serrer les freins.

branch, la branche.

brassière, le soutien-gorge.

brave, brave, courageux ; **bravely,** bravement, courageusement.

bravo! bravo!

bread, le pain ; **bread-roll,** le petit pain ; **slice of bread,** la tartine ; **stick of bread,** la baguette.

breadth, la largeur.

to **break,** briser, casser ; (*chain, rope, etc.*) rompre (*irr.*) ; **to break out,** éclater, *e.g.* la guerre éclata.

breakdown (*car*), la panne ; **broken-down,** en panne.

breakfast, le petit déjeuner ; **to have breakfast,** déjeuner.

breast, la poitrine, la gorge.

breath, l'haleine (*f.*), le souffle ; **out of breath,** hors d'haleine, essoufflé ; **to regain (recover) one's breath,** reprendre haleine.

to **breathe,** respirer ; **to breathe hard, to blow,** souffler.

breeze, la brise.

Breton, le Breton, *f.* la Bretonne ; (*adj.*) breton.

brick, la brique ; **bricklayer,** le maçon.

bride, la mariée ; **bridegroom,** le marié.

bridge, le pont ; (*ship*) la passerelle.

brief, bref, *f.* brève ; **briefly,** brièvement.

bright, clair ; **brightness,** la clarté; **brilliant,** brillant, éclatant.

to **bring,** 1. (*applying to persons*) amener ; **to bring back (home),** ramener ; **to bring up** (=*rear, train*) élever ; 2. **to bring** (*applying to things*), apporter ; **to bring back (home),** rapporter; **to bring down,** descendre (*with* avoir) ; **to bring up,** monter (*with* avoir) ; **to bring near (up),** approcher, *e.g.* approchez votre chaise ; **to bring in,** rentrer (*with* avoir), *e.g.* j'ai rentré les chaises.

broad, large.
broadcast, une émission.
broken-down (*car*), en panne.
brook, le ruisseau.
broom, le balai.
brother, le frère ; **brother-in-law**, le beau-frère.
brow, le front.
brown, brun ; **brown shoes**, les souliers jaunes.
brush, la brosse ; **tooth-brush**, la brosse à dents ; **to brush**, brosser.
bucket, le seau.
to build, bâtir (finir) ; construire (conduire).
building, le bâtiment, un édifice ; (=*block*) un immeuble.
bull, le taureau.
bullet, la balle.
bullock, le bœuf.
to bump against (into), heurter.
bunch, la grappe, *e.g.* la grappe de raisin ; **bunch of flowers**, le bouquet de fleurs.
burden, le fardeau.
burglar, le cambrioleur.
to burn, brûler.
to burst (*of things inflated*), crever ; (*storms, war, etc.*) éclater ; **to burst out laughing, éclater de rire.**
to bury, enterrer.
bus, un autobus ; **by bus, en** autobus.
bush, le buisson.
business, les affaires (*f.*) ; **mind your own business**, mêlez-vous de ce qui vous regarde.
busy, occupé ; **busy with**, occupé de ; **busy (doing)**, occupé à (faire).
but, mais ; **but for, sans.**
butcher, le boucher ; **butcher's shop, butchery,** la boucherie.
butler, le maître d'hôtel.
butter, le beurre.
butterfly, le papillon.
button, le bouton ; **to button,** boutonner.
to buy, acheter, *e.g.* je lui achète mes légumes.
by, par ; (=*near*) près de ; **just by**, tout près de ; **by the river**, au bord de la rivière ; **to go by**, passer ; **by the way**, à propos ; **to recognize by**, reconnaître à, *e.g.* je l'ai reconnu à sa voix.

C

cabbage, le chou, *pl.* les choux.
café, le café.
cage, la cage.
cake, le gâteau.
to calculate, calculer.
calculated to (do), propre à (faire).
calf, le veau.
call, un appel ; (=*errand*) la course ; **to pay some calls**, faire des courses.
to call, appeler ; **to call back**, rappeler ; **I am called X**, je m'appelle X ; **to call (cry) out**, crier ; **to call on** (*a person*), rendre visite à, passer chez, *e.g.* j'ai rendu visite à X, j'ai passé chez X.
calm, calme.
camera, un appareil (photographique) ; **cine-camera**, la caméra.
to camp, camper, faire du camping ; **camping**, le camping.
can, *expressed by* pouvoir (*irr.*) ; **he can walk**, il peut marcher ; **he could walk**, il pouvait marcher ; **can** (=*to know how*) *expressed by* savoir, *e.g.* il sait nager (danser, conduire une auto, etc.).

Canada, le Canada ; **in** (*or* **to**) **Canada**, au Canada ; **Canadian**, le Canadien, *f.* la Canadienne.
candid, franc, *f.* franche.
candle, la bougie, la chandelle.
candy (=*sweet*), le bonbon.
canvas, la toile.
cap (*peaked*), la casquette.
capital (city), la capitale.
captain, le capitaine.
car, une auto(mobile), la voiture ; **by car**, en auto, en voiture.
card, la carte ; **postcard**, la carte postale ; **to play cards**, jouer aux cartes.
cardboard, le carton ; **cardboard box**, le carton.
care (=*attentiveness*), le soin ; **to take care of**, avoir soin de ; **care** (=*trouble*, *worry*), le souci ; **to care about**, se soucier de.
careful (=*attentive*), soigneux ; **carefully**, soigneusement, avec soin ; **careful** (=*prudent*), prudent ; **be careful!** attention! prenez garde! **to be careful not to (do)**, se garder de (faire), prendre garde de (faire), *e.g.* gardez-vous (prenez garde) de tomber.
careless, négligent ; **carelessly**, négligemment ; **carelessness**, la négligence.
caretaker, le (la) concierge.
careworn, soucieux.
carpet, le tapis.
carriage, la voiture ; (*railway*) le wagon.
carrot, la carotte.
to **carry**, porter ; **to carry away (off)**, emporter.
cart, la charrette.
cartridge, la cartouche.

F

case, le cas ; **in any case**, en tout cas ; (=*suitcase*) la valise.
cash, l'argent comptant ; **cash-desk**, la caisse.
castle, le château ; (*fortified*) le château fort.
cat, le chat.
to **catch**, attraper ; **to catch a train**, prendre un train ; **to catch a fish**, prendre un poisson.
cathedral, la cathédrale.
cattle, le bétail.
cauliflower, le chou-fleur.
cave, la caverne, la grotte.
to **cease**, cesser (de); **without ceasing**, sans cesse.
ceiling, le plafond.
to **celebrate**, célébrer, fêter ; **celebrated**, célèbre ; **celebration**, la fête.
cellar, la cave.
cemetery, le cimetière.
central heating, le chauffage central.
centre, le centre ; **in the centre of**, au centre de.
century, le siècle ; **in the twentieth century**, au vingtième siècle.
ceremony, la cérémonie.
certain, certain ; **certainly**, certainement ; **certain people**, certaines personnes ; **certain death**, la mort certaine.
chain, la chaîne.
chair, la chaise.
chalk, la craie.
chance (=*opportunity*), une occasion ; **by chance**, par hasard.
to **change**, changer ; **I change my shoes**, je change de souliers.
change (=*alteration*), le changement ; (*money*) la monnaie, *e.g.* voulez-vous me donner la monnaie de dix francs ?

Channel ; **English Channel,** la Manche ; **Channel Islands,** les îles Anglo-normandes.
chapter, le chapitre.
character, le caractère ; (*in a play*) le personnage.
charge ; **to take charge of,** se charger de.
to charge (*money*), prendre, demander, *e.g.* ils lui ont demandé (pris) dix francs.
charming, charmant.
charwoman, la femme de ménage.
to chase, poursuivre (suivre).
to chat, causer.
to chatter, bavarder.
chauffeur, le chauffeur.
cheap, peu cher ; bon marché (*invar.*).
to cheat, tricher.
cheek, la joue.
to cheer (**up**), égayer, réjouir (finir) ; **cheerful,** joyeux, gai.
cheese, le fromage.
chemist, le pharmacien ; **chemist's shop,** la pharmacie.
cherry, la cerise ; **cherry-tree,** le cerisier.
chest, la poitrine.
chestnut (*edible*), la châtaigne ; **chestnut-tree,** le châtaignier ; **horse-chestnut,** le marron d'Inde ; **horse-chestnut tree,** le marronnier d'Inde.
chick, le poussin ; **chicken,** le poulet ; **chicken-house,** le poulailler.
chief, le chef ; **chief** (*adj.*), principal.
child, un(e) enfant ; **childhood,** l'enfance (*f.*).
chilly, frais, *f.* fraîche.
chimney, la cheminée.
chocolate, le chocolat.
choice, le choix.
choir, le chœur.
to choose, choisir (finir).
to chop, couper; **to chop off,** trancher.
chop (*of meat*), la côtelette.
Christmas, (la) Noël.
church, une église.
cicada, la cigale.
cider, le cidre.
cigarette, la cigarette ; **cigarette-case,** un étui.
cinema, le cinéma.
circle, le cercle.
citizen, le citoyen, *f.* la citoyenne.
city, la ville.
clad in, vêtu de, habillé de.
to claim (=*demand*), réclamer ; (=*assert*) prétendre (vendre).
to clap (**one's hands**), battre des mains ; applaudir (finir).
class, la classe ; **first-class** (*adj.*), de première classe ; **classroom,** la salle de classe.
clean, propre, *e.g.* un visage propre ; **to clean,** nettoyer ; (*shoes*) cirer.
clear, clair ; **clearly,** clairement ; **I see clearly,** j'y vois clair.
to cleave, fendre (vendre).
clerk, un employé.
clever, intelligent, habile.
client, le client, *f.* la cliente.
cliff, la falaise.
to climb (=*clamber*), grimper dans *or* sur, *e.g.* il grimpa dans (sur) un arbre ; (=*to walk up*) gravir (finir), *e.g.* il gravit la montagne.
cloakroom (=*luggage room*), la consigne.
clock (*public*), une horloge ; (*in house*) la pendule ; **to wind**

up the clock, remonter la pendule.

clog, le sabot.

to close, fermer ; **the door closes,** la porte se ferme ; **to close again,** refermer.

close to, près de ; **closely,** de près, *e.g.* il me regarda de près.

clothes, les habits (*m.*), les vêtements (*m.*).

cloud, le nuage ; **cloudless,** sans nuages, pur.

clumsy, maladroit.

coach (*railway*), le wagon ; **stage-coach,** la diligence ; **coachman,** le cocher.

coal, le charbon.

coast, la côte.

coat (=*jacket*), le veston ; (*man's overcoat*) le pardessus ; (*woman's coat*) le manteau ; **frock-coat,** la redingote.

cobbler, le cordonnier.

cock, le coq.

coffee, le café ; **coffee-pot,** la cafetière.

coin, la pièce (de monnaie).

cold, froid ; **it (the weather) is cold,** il fait froid ; **I am cold,** j'ai froid ; **the water is cold,** l'eau est froide ; **I have a cold,** je suis enrhumé ; **I catch cold,** je prends froid.

to collapse, s'écrouler, s'effondrer.

collar, le faux-col.

colleague, le collègue, le confrère.

to collect (*e.g. stamps*), collectionner ; (=*assemble*) s'assembler, *e.g.* une foule s'assembla.

to collide with (*e.g.* a wall), heurter ; (*vehicles*) entrer en collision avec.

colour, la couleur.

comb, le peigne ; **to comb one's hair,** se peigner.

combine harvester , la moissonneuse-batteuse.

to come, venir (*irr., conj. with* être) ; **to come in,** entrer (*with* être) ; **to come out,** sortir (*with* être) ; **to come up,** monter (*with* être) ; **to come up to** (=*approach*), s'approcher de ; **to come down,** descendre (*with* être) ; **to come forward,** s'avancer ; **to come after,** suivre, succéder à ; **come on!** allons! **come now!** allons! voyons! **comings and goings,** les allées et venues.

to comfort, consoler.

comfortable (*chairs, etc.*), confortable ; (*of persons*) à l'aise, à son aise ; **I am comfortable here,** je suis bien ici.

to command, commander, *e.g.* il lui commanda de se lever.

to commence, commencer, *e.g.* ils commencent à jouer.

commercial traveller, le voyageur de commerce.

common, commun ; **commonly,** communément.

companion, le compagnon, *f.* la compagne.

company, la compagnie ; la société.

compartment, le compartiment.

to compel, forcer, contraindre (craindre) ; **they forced me to do it,** ils me forcèrent à le faire ; **I am forced to do it,** je suis forcé de le faire.

competition, le concours.

to complain, se plaindre (craindre).

complaint (=*illness*), la maladie, le mal.

complete, complet, *f.* complète.

to complete, compléter, achever.
complexion, le teint.
compliment, le compliment ; **to pay compliments**, faire des compliments.
composition, la composition.
comrade, le (la) camarade.
to conceal, cacher.
conceited, orgueilleux.
to conceive, concevoir (recevoir).
concert, le concert.
to conclude, conclure (*irr.*).
condition, la condition, un état.
conduct, la conduite.
to conduct, conduire (*irr.*); **to conduct oneself**, se conduire.
conductor (*bus, etc.*), le receveur; (*music*) le chef d'orchestre.
confectioner, le confiseur ; **confectioner's shop**, la confiserie.
to confess, avouer ; **confession**, un aveu.
confidence, la confiance.
conflagration, un incendie.
to confuse, confondre (vendre).
confused, confus.
confusion, la confusion, le trouble.
to congratulate (on), féliciter (de) ; **congratulations**, les félicitations (*f.*).
to conquer, conquérir (acquérir) ; **conquest**, la conquête.
to consent, consentir (dormir).
consequently, par conséquent.
to consider, considérer.
to consist of, consister en, *e.g.* la maison consiste en six pièces ; **to consist in (doing)**, consister à (faire).
to console, consoler.
constable (*police*), un agent de police (*town*), le gendarme (*country*).
constantly, constamment.
to construct, construire (conduire) ; **construction**, la construction.
to consult, consulter.
to contain, contenir (tenir) ; renfermer.
to contemn, mépriser.
contempt, le mépris.
content, content ; **to content oneself with (doing)**, se contenter de (faire).
continually, continuellement, sans cesse.
to continue, continuer, *e.g.* je continue à leur écrire.
contrary ; **on the contrary**, au contraire.
convenient, commode.
convent, le couvent.
conversation, la conversation, un entretien.
to converse, causer.
to convince, convaincre (vaincre).
to cook, cuire ; **I cook the meat**, je fais cuire la viande ; **cooked**, cuit ; **cooking**, la - cuisine ; **cook** (*person*), le cuisinier, *f.* la cuisinière; **gas cooker**, la cuisinière à gaz; **electric cooker**, la cuisinière électrique.
cool, frais, *f.* fraîche.
to cool, refroidir (finir).
cork, le bouchon ; **cork-screw**, le tire-bouchon.
corn, le blé.
corner, le coin.
corpse, le cadavre.
correct, correct, exact.
correspondence, la correspondance; (*mail*) le courrier; **correspondent**, le correspondant.
corridor, le couloir, le corridor.
to cost, coûter ; **to cost dear (a lot)**, coûter cher ; **at all costs**, à tout prix ; **costly**, coûteux.
costume, le costume.

cottage (*thatched*), la chaumière.
cough, la toux ; **to cough**, tousser.
could ; he could (=*was able*), il pouvait ; **he could** (=*would be able*), il pourrait ; **he could have waited**, il aurait pu attendre.
to count, compter.
counter, le comptoir.
country (=*land*), le pays ; (*patriotic sense*) la patrie ; (=*countryside*) la campagne ; **in the country**, à la campagne ; **countryman**, le paysan ; **countrywoman**, la paysanne ; **fellow-countryman**, le compatriote ; **fellow-countrywoman**, la compatriote ; **country house** (**mansion**), le château.
courage, le courage ; **to pluck up one's courage**, prendre son courage à deux mains ; **courageous**, courageux.
of course, bien entendu, évidemment, naturellement, bien sûr ; **why, of course!** parbleu!
courteous, courtois.
courtyard, la cour.
cousin, le cousin, *f.* la cousine.
to cover, couvrir (ouvrir) ; (*distance*) parcourir ; **covered with**, couvert de.
cow, la vache ; **cow-shed**, une étable.
coward, le lâche ; **cowardly**, lâche.
cracked, fêlé.
cradle, le berceau.
crafty, rusé
crash (*noise*), le fracas.
to creak, grincer.
cream, la crème.
creature, la bête.
to creep, ramper ; **to creep into**, se glisser dans.
cricket (*insect*), le grillon.
cricket (*game*), le cricket ; **to play cricket**, jouer au cricket.
crime, le crime.
crocks, crockery, la vaisselle.
crop, la récolte.
cross, la croix ; **to cross** (*two things*), croiser ; (=*go across*) traverser, (*hills, rivers*) franchir (finir) ; **crossroads**, le carrefour, le croisement de rues (de routes).
crouching, accroupi, blotti.
crow, le corbeau.
crowd, la foule ; **in a crowd, in crowds**, en foule.
cruel, cruel, *f.* cruelle ; **cruelty**, la cruauté.
crumb, la miette.
to crush, écraser.
crust, la croûte.
to cry (=*weep*), pleurer ; (=*cry out*) crier ; (=*exclaim*) s'écrier.
cry, le cri ; **to utter a cry**, pousser un cri.
to cultivate, cultiver.
cunning, rusé, fin.
cup, la tasse.
cupboard, une armoire, un placard.
to cure, guérir (finir).
curious, curieux.
current, le courant.
curtain, le rideau.
cushion, le coussin.
custom, la coutume.
customer, le client, *f.* la cliente.
customs, la douane ; **customs-officer**, le douanier.
to cut, couper ; **to cut down**, couper, abattre (battre).
to cycle, aller (rouler) à bicyclette ;

I cycle to school, je vais à l'école à bicyclette.

cyclist, le cycliste.

D

dagger, le poignard.

daily, quotidien (*f.* -ienne), journalier ; **daily help** (*charwoman*), la femme de ménage.

to damage, endommager, abîmer.

dance (=*dancing*), la danse ; (=*party, ball*) le bal ; **to dance,** danser ; **dancer,** le danseur, *f.* la danseuse.

danger, le danger ; **in danger,** en danger ; **dangerous,** dangereux.

to dare, oser, *e.g.* j'ose parler.

dark (*person*), brun ; (*colour*) foncé ; (=*without light*), sombre, obscur ; **it is dark,** il fait sombre ; il fait nuit ; **it is pitch-dark,** il fait nuit noire ; **darkness,** l'obscurité (*f.*), l'ombre (*f.*).

to dash (forward), s'élancer, se précipiter.

date, la date, *e.g.* quelle date sommes-nous aujourd'hui ?

daughter, la fille ; **daughter-in-law,** la bru.

dawn, l'aube (*f.*), le point du jour.

day, le jour ; (*as in "a busy day", etc.*) la journée ; **good day,** bonjour, (*leaving*) au revoir ; **every day,** tous les jours ; **daybreak,** l'aube (*f.*), le point du jour ; **in our day,** de nos jours ; **in the old days,** autrefois, jadis ; **a day off, a day's holiday,** un jour de congé ; **I have done nothing all day,** je n'ai rien fait de la journée.

to dazzle, éblouir (finir).

dead, mort.

deaf, sourd.

deal ; a good deal (of), beaucoup (de).

dear, cher, *f.* chère.

death, la mort.

to deceive, tromper.

December, décembre (*m.*) ; **in December,** en décembre, au mois de décembre.

decent, honnête, brave, convenable.

to decide to (do), décider de (faire), *e.g.* j'ai décidé de rester.

decidedly, décidément.

deck, le pont.

to declare, déclarer.

deed, un acte, une action ; (*heroic*) un exploit.

deep (*sea*), l'abîme (*m.*).

deep (*adj.*), profond ; **deeply,** profondément.

defeat, la défaite ; **to defeat,** vaincre (*irr.*).

to defend, défendre (vendre).

delay, le retard ; **to delay,** retarder, *e.g.* cet incident retarda notre départ.

delicacy (*to eat*), la friandise.

delicate, délicat.

delicious, délicieux.

to delight, ravir (finir), enchanter ; **delighted,** ravi, enchanté, *e.g.* je suis enchanté de vous voir ; **delightful,** délicieux.

to demand, exiger.

to demolish, démolir (finir).

dentist, le dentiste.

to depart, partir (*with* être) ; **departure,** le départ.

to depend, dépendre (vendre) ; **that (it) depends,** cela dépend.

to deprive (of), priver (de).

to descend, descendre (vendre) (*conj. with* être).
to describe, décrire (écrire) ; **description**, la description.
desert, le désert.
deserted, désert, *e.g.* les rues désertes.
to deserve, mériter, *e.g.* vous méritez de réussir.
design, le dessin.
desire, le désir, une envie ; **to desire**, désirer, *e.g.* je désire voir le directeur.
desk (*school*), le pupitre ; (*master's*) la chaire ; (*office, study*) le bureau.
despair, le désespoir ; **to despair**, désespérer ; **desperate**, désespéré.
to despise, mépriser.
dessert, le dessert.
destination, la destination.
to destroy, détruire (conduire).
detail, le détail, *pl.* les détails.
to detest, détester.
to devote (*e.g. time, energy*), consacrer.
devoted, dévoué ; **devotion**, le dévouement.
to devour, dévorer.
dew, la rosée.
to die, mourir (*irr.*) ; **he has died**, il est mort.
different, différent ; **difference**, la différence.
difficult, difficile ; **difficulty**, la difficulté ; **without any difficulty**, sans aucune difficulté ; **I got him out of his difficulty**, je le tirai d'embarras.
to dig (*e.g. a hole*), creuser ; **to dig (thrust) in**, enfoncer.
digestion, la digestion.
dignified, digne.
dim (*light*), faible ; (*eyes*) trouble.
to dine, dîner ; **dining-room**, la salle à manger ; **dining-car**, le wagon-restaurant.
dinner (*midday*), le déjeuner ; (*evening*) le dîner ; **to have dinner**, dîner ; (=*ceremonial dinner*) le banquet.
by dint of, à force de.
direction, la direction ; le côté ; **in** (*or* **from**) **the direction of the station**, du côté de la gare ; le sens, *e.g.* il marchait dans le sens contraire.
dirty, sale.
disadvantage, un inconvénient.
disagreeable, désagréable.
to disappear, disparaître (connaître) ; **disappearance**, la disparition.
to disappoint, décevoir (recevoir), désappointer ; **disappointed**, déçu, désappointé ; **disappointment**, la déception, le désappointement.
to discourage, décourager ; **to be discouraged**, se décourager.
to discover, découvrir (ouvrir) ; **discovery**, la découverte.
to discuss, discuter.
disdain, le dédain ; **to disdain**, dédaigner.
to disembark, débarquer.
to disguise, déguiser ; **disguised as**, déguisé en.
disgusting, dégoûtant.
dish, le plat ; **dish-washer**, le lave-vaisselle.
to dismiss, renvoyer, congédier.
to dismount, descendre de cheval, mettre pied à terre.
to disobey, désobéir (finir), *e.g.* il leur désobéit.
disorder, le désordre.
to display, étaler.
to displease, déplaire (plaire), *e.g.*

cela déplaît au directeur ; **displeased (with)**, mécontent (de).

disposal ; he has a large sum of money at his disposal, il dispose d'une grosse somme d'argent.

disposed to (do), disposé à (faire), enclin à (faire).

dissatisfied, mécontent.

distance, la distance ; **some distance away,** à quelque distance ; **in the distance,** au loin.

distant, lointain.

distinct, distinct ; **distinctly,** distinctement.

to distinguish, distinguer.

distress, la détresse, l'angoisse (*f.*) ; **distressing,** pénible.

district (*of a town*), le quartier ; (*of a country*) la région, le pays.

to distrust, se méfier de ; **distrustful,** méfiant.

to disturb, déranger ; (=*to make anxious*) inquiéter ; **disturbing,** inquiétant.

ditch, le fossé.

to dive, plonger.

to divide, diviser ; **to divide into 3 parts,** diviser en trois parties.

to do, faire ; **what are you going to do with this money?** qu'allez-vous faire de cet argent ?

dcctor, le médecin, le docteur.

dog, le chien.

doll, la poupée.

domestic (*adj.*), domestique.

donkey, un âne.

door, la porte ; (*of a vehicle*) la portière ; **front (street) door,** la porte d'entrée ; **doorway, big doors,** le portail ; **doorstep,** le pas de la porte, le seuil ; **door-knocker,** le marteau ; **door-keeper,** le (la) concierge, le portier ; **they live next door,** ils habitent à côté.

dormitory, le dortoir.

doubt, le doute ; **without doubt,** sans doute ; **to doubt,** douter.

down ; to fall down (*a pit, well, etc.*), tomber dans ; **the water was running down the wall,** l'eau coulait le long du mur ; **to put down,** déposer ; **to take (bring) down,** descendre (*with* avoir) ; **to go (come) down,** descendre (*with* être) ; **to bend down,** se baisser, **to lie down,** se coucher ; **downpour** (*of rain*), une averse ; **downstairs,** en bas ; **down-hearted,** abattu.

to doze, s'assoupir (finir), sommeiller.

dozen, la douzaine.

to drag, traîner ; **to drag away,** entraîner.

dragon-fly, la libellule.

draught, le courant d'air.

to draw (=*pull*), tirer, traîner ; (=*make a picture*) dessiner ; **to draw out,** retirer ; **to draw near (to),** s'approcher (de).

drawer, le tiroir.

drawing, le dessin ; **drawing-room,** le salon.

dread, l'effroi (*m.*) ; **dreadful,** effroyable ; **to dread,** redouter.

dream, le rêve ; **to dream,** rêver.

dress, la robe ; (*general*) la tenue ; **to dress (oneself),** s'habiller ; **dressed in,** habillé de, vêtu de ; **dressing-gown,** la robe de chambre ; **dressing-table,** la table de toilette ; **dressmaking,** la couture ; **dressmaker,** le couturier, *f.* la couturière.

to drink, boire (*irr.*) ; **drink,** la boisson.

to drive, conduire (*irr.*) ; **to drive in** (*stakes, etc.*) enfoncer ;

driver, le conducteur, le chauffeur ; **drive** (*through park etc.*), une allée.

drop, la goutte ; **to drop** (=*fall*), tomber ; (=*let fall*) laisser tomber.

drowned, noyé ; **to be drowned,** se noyer.

drowsy, assoupi.

druggist, le pharmacien ; **drug-store,** la pharmacie.

drum, le tambour.

drunk, ivre.

dry, sec, *f.* sèche ; **to dry,** sécher.

duck, le canard.

dumb, muet, *f.* muette.

during, pendant.

dust, la poussière ; **dusty,** poussiéreux, poudreux ; **to dust,** épousseter.

Dutch, hollandais ; **Dutchman, -woman,** le (la) Hollandais(e).

to **dwell,** demeurer ; **dwelling,** la demeure, le logis.

E

each (*adj.*), chaque, *e.g.* chaque personne ; **each** (one) (*pronoun*), chacun, *f.* chacune ; **they look at each other,** ils se regardent.

ear, une oreille.

early, de bonne heure ; **early in the morning,** de bon (grand) matin ; le matin, de bonne heure ; **so early,** si tôt, de si bonne heure ; **too early,** trop tôt.

to **earn,** gagner ; **to earn one's living,** gagner sa vie.

earnest, sérieux ; **earnestly,** sérieusement.

earth, la terre.

ease, l'aise (*f.*) ; **at my ease,** à mon aise, à l'aise ; **to ease** (*pain, etc.*), soulager.

east, l'est (*m.*).

Easter, Pâques ; **Easter holidays,** les vacances de Pâques.

easy, facile ; **easily,** facilement ; **easy chair,** le fauteuil ; **easy-going,** indulgent.

to **eat,** manger ; **to eat heartily,** manger de bon appétit.

edge, le bord.

egg, un œuf.

either, non plus ; **John won't come either,** Jean ne viendra pas non plus.

to **elapse,** s'écouler, *e.g.* les années s'écoulèrent.

elbow, le coude.

elder, aîné(e) ; **eldest,** l'aîné(e).

electric bulb, une ampoule électrique.

electricity, l'électricité (*f.*).

elevator (=*lift*), un ascenseur.

elm, un orme.

else ; **someone else,** quelqu'un d'autre ; **nobody else,** personne d'autre ; **somewhere else, elsewhere,** ailleurs ; **something else,** autre chose.

to **embark,** s'embarquer.

to **embarrass,** embarrasser, gêner ; **embarrassment,** l'embarras (*m.*), la gêne.

emperor, l'empereur ; **empress,** l'impératrice.

to **employ,** employer ; **employer,** le patron.

empty, vide ; **to empty,** vider ; **the church empties,** l'église se vide.

to **enable,** permettre (mettre), *e.g.* cela leur permit de partir.

to **enclose,** renfermer.

to **encounter,** rencontrer ; **encounter,** la rencontre.

to **encourage,** encourager (à).

end (*of an event, story, etc.*), la fin ; (*of a thing*) le bout ; (= *far end*) le fond, *e.g.* au fond du jardin ; **at the end of six months,** au bout de six mois ; **to put an end to,** mettre fin à, *e.g.* cela mit fin à leur discussion ; **to end,** finir, terminer.

to **endure,** supporter.

enemy, un ennemi.

engine (*motor*), le moteur ; **to start up the engine,** mettre le moteur en marche.

England, l'Angleterre (*f.*) ; **in** (*or* **to**) **England,** en Angleterre ; **English,** anglais ; **Englishman,** un Anglais ; **Englishwoman,** une Anglaise ; **English boy,** le jeune (petit) Anglais ; **English girl,** la jeune (petite) Anglaise ; **English Channel,** la Manche.

to **enjoy,** jouir (finir) *e.g.* nous jouissons de notre liberté ; **to enjoy oneself,** s'amuser.

enormous, énorme ; **enormously,** énormément.

enough, assez, *e.g.* assez de lait ; **to be enough,** suffire (*irr.*).

to **enquire about,** s'informer de ; **an enquiry,** un renseignement ; **to make enquiries,** se renseigner, demander des renseignements.

to **enrich,** enrichir (finir).

to **enter,** entrer (*with* être) ; **he entered the house,** il entra dans la maison.

entertainment, un amusement, le divertissement, la distraction.

entire, entier, *f.* entière.

entrance, une entrée ; **entrance hall,** le vestibule.

to **entreat,** implorer, supplier.

to **entrust,** charger, *e.g.* il m'a chargé d'une commission.

entry, une entrée.

to **envelop,** envelopper.

envelope, une enveloppe.

envy, l'envie (*f.*) ; **to envy,** envier, *e.g.* je lui envie son bonheur.

erect, droit.

errand, la commission ; **I run** (**do**) **some errands,** je fais des commissions.

escape, une évasion ; **to escape** (=*avoid*), échapper, *e.g.* il échappa à la mort ; (=*get out*) s'évader, s'échapper (de), *e.g.* il s'échappa de sa prison.

especially, surtout.

to **establish,** établir (finir) ; **establishment,** un établissement.

estate (*country*), la propriété.

Europe, l'Europe (*f.*) ; **European,** l'Européen, *f.* l'Européenne.

eve (=*day before*), la veille ; **Christmas Eve,** la veille de Noël.

even (*adv.*), même.

evening, le soir ; (*as in* "*a pleasant evening,*" *etc.*) la soirée ; **good evening,** bonsoir ; **Friday evening,** vendredi soir ; **the evening before,** la veille (au soir).

event, un événement.

ever, jamais ; **not ever,** ne ... jamais ; **for ever,** pour toujours.

every, chaque, *e.g.* chaque personne ; **every day** (**month,** *etc.*), tous les jours (mois, etc.) **everybody,** tout le monde ; **everything,** tout ; **everywhere,** partout.

evident, évident ; **evidently,** évidemment.

ewe, la brebis.

exact, exact, juste; **exactly**, exactement, juste, justement; **at exactly 3 o'clock**, à trois heures précises.

examination, un examen.

to examine, examiner.

example, un exemple; **for example**, par exemple.

to exceed, dépasser.

excellent, excellent, *e.g.* un excellent repas.

except, excepté, sauf.

to exchange, échanger, *e.g.* ils ont échangé leur maison contre un appartement.

excited, ému; **exciting**, émouvant, passionnant; **excitement**, l'émotion (*f.*), l'émoi (*m.*).

to exclaim, s'écrier, s'exclamer.

excuse, une excuse; **to excuse**, excuser; **to excuse oneself**, s'excuser; **excuse me**, excusez-moi; pardon.

to exercise, exercer.

exercise book, le cahier.

to exhaust, épuiser; **exhausted**, épuisé.

to exist, exister; **existence**, l'existence (*f.*)

exit, la sortie.

to expect, compter, *e.g.* je compte vous voir demain; s'attendre à, *e.g.* je m'attendais à cette réponse; je ne m'attendais pas à vous voir.

expectation, une attente.

to expend, dépenser; **expense**, **expenditure**, la dépense, les frais (*m.*); **they were laughing at my expense**, ils riaient à mes dépens; **expensive**, cher, coûteux.

experience, l'expérience (*f.*); **to experience** (*feelings, etc.*), éprouver.

experiment, une expérience.

to explain, expliquer.

to explore, explorer.

to expose, exposer.

to express, exprimer; **expression**, une expression (*f.*).

express (*train*), le rapide.

exquisite, exquis.

to extend, (s')étendre (vendre), *e.g.* la plaine s'étend au loin.

to extinguish, éteindre (craindre).

extraordinary, extraordinaire.

extreme, extrême; **extremely**, extrêmement.

eye, un œil, *pl.* des yeux; **he opened his eyes wide**, il ouvrit de grands (gros) yeux; **eyebrow**, le sourcil; **eyelid**, la paupière; **eyelash**, le cil.

F

face, le visage, la figure.

fact, le fait; **in fact**, en effet; **as a matter of fact**, à vrai dire.

factory, une usine, la fabrique.

to fade (*of flowers, etc.*), se faner, se flétrir (finir); (*from hearing or sight*) se perdre (vendre).

to fail, échouer.

failing, le défaut.

faint (*sound, etc.*), léger.

to faint, s'évanouir (finir); **fainting**, **fainted**, évanoui.

fair (*trading*), la foire.

fair (*adj.*), juste, loyal; (*hair*) blond.

fairly, assez, *e.g.* assez difficile.

fairy, la fée.

faithful, fidèle.

to fall, tomber (*with* être); **to fall down** (=*collapse*), s'écrouler, s'effondrer.

false, faux, *f.* fausse.

familiar, familier.

family, la famille.

famished, affamé.

famous, célèbre, fameux.

fancy that! par exemple!

far (*adj.*), lointain, *e.g.* les collines lointaines ; (*adv.*) loin ; **far away,** au loin ; **far from,** loin de ; **not far from,** non loin de ; **as far as,** aussi loin que, (=*up to*) jusqu'à ; **how far is it from here to Paris?** Combien (*or* Quelle distance) y a-t-il d'ici à Paris?

farewell, adieu ; **to say one's farewells,** faire ses adieux.

farm, la ferme ; **farm-yard,** la cour de ferme, la basse-cour ; **farmer,** le fermier ; **farmer's wife,** la fermière.

fashion (=*way*), la façon ; (*clothes, etc.*) la mode ; **in the fashion,** à la mode ; **fashionable** (*resorts, etc.*), mondain.

fast, rapide ; (*adv.*) vite, rapidement.

to fasten, attacher.

fat, gras, *f.* grasse.

fate, le destin, le sort ; (*person's fate*) le sort.

father, le père ; **Father** (*fam.*), papa ; **father-in-law,** le beau-père.

fatherland, la patrie.

fault, la faute ; (=*failing*) le défaut.

favourite, favori, *f.* favorite ; préféré, *e.g.* mes livres préférés.

to fear, avoir peur, craindre (*irr.*), *e.g.* j'ai peur de le faire, je crains de le faire ; **fear,** la peur, la crainte ; **for fear of (doing),** de peur de (faire) ; **for fear that,** de peur que +*subj. with* ne, *e.g.* de peur qu'il ne nous voie.

feast-day (*church*), la fête.

February, février ; **in February,** en février, au mois de février.

to feed, nourrir (finir) ; donner à manger à, *e.g.* j'ai donné à manger aux chats.

to feel, sentir (dormir) ; (*emotions, sensations*) éprouver, ressentir ; **she felt miserable,** elle se sentait malheureuse ; **I feel like resting,** j'ai envie de me reposer.

feeling, le sentiment.

to feign, feindre (craindre), *e.g.* il feignit de me croire.

to fell (*trees*), couper, abattre (battre).

fellow ; young fellow, le garçon, le jeune homme ; **young fellows,** les jeunes gens ; **old fellow,** le (vieux) bonhomme ; **a good fellow,** un brave homme (garçon) ; **fellow-countryman,** le compatriote.

ferocious, féroce.

to fetch, aller chercher.

fête, la fête.

fever, la fièvre ; **feverish,** fiévreux.

few, peu (de), *e.g.* peu d'arbres ; **fewer,** moins (de), *e.g.* moins d'arbres ; **a few minutes,** quelques minutes.

field (*cultivated*), le champ ; (*grass*) le pré, la prairie.

to fight, se battre, combattre.

figure (*number*), le chiffre ; (*body*) la taille ; (*human form that looms up*) la silhouette.

to file past (by), défiler.

to fill, emplir (finir), remplir (finir) ; **filled with,** rempli de.

film, le film.

finally, enfin.

to find, trouver ; **to find again,** retrouver.

fine, beau (bel *before a vowel*), *f.* belle ; **it (the weather) is fine**, il fait beau.

finger, le doigt ; **finger-nail**, un ongle.

to **finish**, achever, finir.

fir (-tree), le sapin.

fire, le feu (*pl.* -x) ; (=*conflagration*) un incendie ; **to light a fire**, allumer du feu ; **to catch fire**, prendre feu ; **at (by) the fireside**, au coin du feu ; **fireplace**, la cheminée ; **fireman**, le pompier ; **fire engine**, la pompe à incendie ; **to fire a shot**, tirer un coup de feu (de fusil).

firm, ferme, solide.

first, premier, *f.* première ; **at first, first of all**, d'abord.

fish, le poisson ; **fishing**, la pêche : **fishing rod**, la canne à pêche ; **to fish**, pêcher ; **to go fishing**, aller à la pêche ; **fisherman**, le pêcheur ; **fishing boat**, la barque de pêche.

fist, le poing.

to **fix**, fixer.

flag, le drapeau.

flagstone, la dalle.

flat, un appartement.

flat (*adj.*), plat.

to **flatter**, flatter.

flea, la puce.

to **flee**, fuir (*irr.*), s'enfuir.

flesh, la chair.

flight (*on wings*), **le vol** ; (= *escape*) la fuite.

float (*fishing*), le flotteur.

to **float**, flotter.

flock (*of sheep*), le troupeau.

floor (*boarded*), le plancher, (*block*) le parquet ; (*of building*) un étage ; **on the first floor**, au premier étage ; **ground-floor**, le rez-de-chaussée.

florist, le (la) fleuriste.

flour, la farine.

to **flow**, couler.

flower, la fleur ; **flower-bed**, la plate-bande, *pl.* les plates-bandes ; le parterre.

fluent, courant ; **fluently**, couramment.

fly, la mouche.

to **fly**, voler ; **to fly away**, s'envoler.

fog, le brouillard ; **it is foggy**, il fait du brouillard ; **the fog clears**, le brouillard se dissipe.

to **fold**, plier.

foliage, le feuillage.

folk, les gens.

to **follow**, suivre (*irr.*) ; **followed by**, suivi de ; **following**, suivant ; **the following day**, le lendemain ; **the following morning**, le lendemain matin.

folly, la folie.

fond ; **to be (very) fond of**, aimer beaucoup.

food, la nourriture.

fool, un imbécile, un sot ; **foolish**, sot, *f.* sotte ; stupide ; **foolishness**, la sottise, la stupidité.

foot, le pied ; (*of an animal*) la patte ; **on foot**, à pied ; **footstep**, le pas ; **footprint**, une empreinte de pied ; **footbridge**, la passerelle ; **footman**, le valet de pied ; **football**, le football ; **to play football**, jouer au football.

for (*conj.*), car ; (*prep.*) pour ; (=*during*) pendant, *e.g.* nous avons joué pendant une heure ; **to send for**, envoyer chercher.

to **forbid**, défendre (vendre), *e.g.* je lui défends de le faire ; **it is forbidden to (do)**, il est défendu de (faire).

to **force**, forcer, *e.g.* ils me forcèrent à accepter ; je suis forcé d'accepter.
forehead, le front.
foreign, étranger, *f.* -ère ; **foreigner**, un étranger, *f.* une étrangère.
forest, la forêt.
to **forget**, oublier, *e.g.* j'ai oublié de fermer les fenêtres.
to **forgive**, pardonner, *e.g.* je lui pardonne sa faute ; **to ask forgiveness**, demander pardon.
fork, la fourchette.
form, la forme ; **to form**, former.
former, ancien, *f.* ancienne, *e.g.* un ancien élève ; **formerly**, autrefois, jadis ; **the former** (*as opposed to* " *the latter* "), celui-là, *f.* celle-là.
formidable, formidable.
forthwith, aussitôt.
fortnight, quinze jours, une quinzaine (de jours).
fortunately, heureusement.
fortune, la fortune ; **he has made a fortune**, il a fait fortune ; **good fortune**, le bonheur ; **by good fortune**, par bonheur.
forward, en avant ; **to go (come) forward**, s'avancer ; **to dash forward**, s'élancer.
foul, sale.
found ; **to be found**, se trouver.
fountain-pen, le stylo.
four, quatre ; **on all fours**, à quatre pattes.
fox, le renard.
frame, le cadre.
franc, le franc.
France, la France ; **to** (*or* **in**) **France**, en France.
frank, franc, *f.* franche ; **frankly**, franchement,
free, libre ; **freedom**, la liberté ; **to free**, libérer.
to **freeze**, geler ; **it is freezing**, il gèle.
French (*language*), le français ; (*adj.*) français ; **Frenchman**, le Français ; **Frenchwoman**, la Française ; **French boy**, le jeune (petit) Français ; **French girl**, la jeune (petite) Française.
frequent, fréquent ; **frequently**, fréquemment ; **to frequent**, fréquenter.
fresh, frais, *f.* fraîche ; **it** (the weather) **is fresh**, il fait frais ; **freshness**, la fraîcheur ; **fresh** (=*new*), nouveau (nouvel *before a vowel*), *f.* nouvelle.
Friday, vendredi (*m.*) ; **Good Friday**, le vendredi saint ; **last Friday**, vendredi dernier ; **next Friday**, vendredi prochain.
friend, un ami, *f.* une amie ; **friendly**, amical ; **friendship**, l'amitié (*f.*).
fright, la frayeur ; **frightful**, affreux, effroyable.
to **frighten**, effrayer, faire peur (à), *e.g.* cela leur fait peur ; **frightening**, effrayant.
frock, la robe ; **frockcoat**, la redingote.
frog, la grenouille.
from, de ; (=*starting from*) à partir de, *e.g.* à partir de demain ; **from day to day**, de jour en jour ; **from house to house**, de maison en maison.
front (*of a building*), la façade ; **in front of**, devant ; **in front** (*adv.*), en avant.
frontier, la frontière.
frost, la gelée.
to **frown**, froncer le sourcil.

frozen, gelé.
fruit, le fruit; **fruit juice**, le jus de fruit; **he sells fruit**, il vend des fruits; **fruit-tree**, le fruitier; **fruit-shop**, la fruiterie; **fruiterer**, le fruitier.
frying-pan, la poêle.
fugitive, le fugitif.
full, plein; **at full speed**, à toute vitesse.
fun; **to make fun of**, se moquer de; **funny**, amusant, drôle.
furious, furieux, *f.* -euse.
to **furnish** (=*supply*), fournir (finir); (=*put in furniture*) meubler; **furnished**, meublé; **furniture**, les meubles (*m.*); **piece of furniture**, le meuble.
furrow, le sillon.
future, futur; (*noun*) l'avenir (*m.*); **in the future**, à l'avenir.

G

gaiety, la gaieté.
gaily, gaiement.
to **gain**, gagner.
gait, la démarche; l'allure (*f.*).
to **gallop**, galoper.
game, le jeu, *pl.* les jeux; **a game of (tennis)**, une partie de (tennis); (=*animals*) le gibier; **game-keeper**, le garde-chasse.
gang, la bande.
gangway (*to ship*), la passerelle.
garage, le garage.
garden, le jardin; **public garden**, le jardin public; **kitchen garden**, le jardin potager; **gardener**, le jardinier.
to **gasp**, haleter.
gate, la porte; (*iron*) la grille; (*farm*) la barrière.
to **gather** (=*pick*), cueillir (*irr.*); (=*assemble*) (s')assembler, (se) rassembler, *e.g.* une foule s'assembla.
gay, gai; **gaily**, gaiement.
to **gaze at**, regarder fixement, contempler, considérer.
general, général; **generally**, généralement, en général.
generous, généreux.
gentle, doux, *f.* douce; **gently**, doucement; **gentleness**, la douceur.
gentleman, le monsieur, *pl.* les messieurs.
Germany, l'Allemagne (*f.*); **German** (*language*), l'allemand; **a German**, un(e) Allemand(e).
gesture, le geste.
to **get**, obtenir (tenir); chercher; **to get up**, se lever; **to get down**, descendre (vendre); **to get home**, rentrer (arriver) à la maison; **to get in**, entrer; **to get into a car**, monter dans une voiture; **to get out of a car**, descendre d'une voiture.
giant, le géant.
gift, le cadeau; **New Year's gift**, les étrennes (*f.*); **to make a gift of**, faire cadeau de, *e.g.* je lui fis cadeau d'un joli collier.
gipsy, le bohémien, *f.* la bohémienne.
girl (*up to* 12-13), la fillette; (*over* 13 *or* 14) la jeune fille.
to **give**, donner; **to give back**, rendre (vendre); **to give up** (=*hand over*), livrer, céder; **to give up** (=*renounce*), renoncer à; **to give out** (*e.g. a scent*), répandre (vendre); **to give away** (=*denounce*), dénoncer.
glad, content, *e.g.* je suis content de vous voir; **gladly**, volontiers; **to gladden**, réjouir

(finir), *e.g.* le soleil les réjouit.

glance, le coup d'œil, le regard; **to glance**, jeter un coup d'œil.

glass, le verre; **glasses** (=*spectacles*), les lunettes (*f.*), les verres.

to glide, glisser.

glimmer, la lueur.

to glisten, étinceler; **glistening**, étincelant.

gloomy, morne; (=*without light*) sombre.

glove, le gant.

glow, la lueur; **to glow**, luire (nuire).

glutton, le gourmand.

to gnaw, ronger.

to go, aller (*with* être); se rendre (vendre); **to go away**, s'en aller; **to go in**, entrer (*with* être); **to go out**, sortir (*with* être), (= *be extinguished*) s'éteindre (craindre); **to go up**, monter (*with* être); **to go up to** (=*approach*), s'approcher de; **to go down**, descendre (*with* être); **to go home**, rentrer (*with* être), rentrer à la maison, rentrer chez soi (moi, nous, etc.); **to go through**, traverser; **to go forward**, s'avancer; **to go towards**, se diriger vers; **to go beyond**, dépasser; **to go on** (=*continue*), continuer, *e.g.* nous continuons à leur écrire; **to go on** (=*resume speaking*), reprendre, continuer; **to go on** (=*happen*), arriver (*with* être), se passer; **to go by**, passer, (*of time*) s'écouler, *e.g.* les jours s'écoulent; **to go with**, accompagner; suivre (*irr.*).

goal, le but.

goat, la chèvre.

gold, l'or (*m.*); **goldfish**, le poisson rouge.

golf, le golf; **to play golf**, jouer au golf; **golf course**, le golf.

good, bon, *f.* bonne; (=*well-behaved*) sage; **good day (morning, afternoon)**, bonjour; **good evening**, bonsoir; **good night**, bonne nuit; **good-bye**, au revoir; **to say good-bye**, faire ses adieux; **to have a good time**, s'amuser bien; **what is the good of waiting?** à quoi bon attendre? **it is no good your (trying)**, vous avez beau (essayer); **Good Friday**, le vendredi saint; **good! that's good!** c'est bien! c'est cela! **good heavens!** mon Dieu!

goodness, la bonté.

goods (*trade*), la marchandise.

goose, une oie.

gorge, la gorge.

to gossip, bavarder.

gown, la robe; **dressing-gown**, la robe de chambre.

gracious me! mon Dieu!

gradually, peu à peu.

gramophone, le gramophone; **gramophone record**, le disque.

grandfather, le grand-père; **grandpa**, grandpapa; **grandmother**, la grand'mère; **grandparents**, les grands-parents; **grandson**, le petit-fils; **granddaughter**, la petite-fille.

grapes, le raisin; **bunch of grapes**, la grappe de raisin.

grass, l'herbe (*f.*).

grasshopper, la sauterelle.

to grate (*sound*), grincer.

grateful (for), reconnaissant (de).

gratitude, la reconnaissance.
grave, grave.
grave (*burial*), la tombe.
to graze (=*eat grass*), paître (connaître) ; brouter (l'herbe) ; (=*just touch*) effleurer.
great, grand.
Great Britain, la Grande-Bretagne.
greatcoat, le pardessus.
greedy, avide ; (*for food*) gourmand.
green, vert.
greengrocer, le marchand de légumes ; (*costermonger*) le marchand des quatre saisons.
greenhouse, la serre.
to greet (=*give a sign of greeting*), saluer ; (=*welcome*) accueillir (cueillir).
grey, gris ; **greying** (*hair*), grisonnant.
to grip, serrer.
to groan, gémir (finir) ; **groan**, le gémissement.
grocer, un épicier ; **grocer's shop**, une épicerie ; **greengrocer**, le marchand de légumes, (=*costermonger*) le marchand des quatre saisons.
grotto, la grotte.
ground, la terre ; (=*soil*) le sol; **on** (*or* **to**) **the ground**, par terre ; **ground floor**, le rez-de-chaussée.
group, le groupe.
to grow, pousser, croître (*irr.*) ; (=*cultivate*) cultiver ; (=*become*) devenir ; **to grow up**, grandir (finir) ; **growing**, grandissant, croissant.
grudge ; **I bear him a grudge**, je lui en veux.
to grumble at, gronder, *e.g.* papa nous a grondés ; **to grumble** (=*speak with ill-grace*), grogner, grommeler.
to grunt, grogner.
to guard, garder.
guard (*train*), le chef de train.
to guess, deviner.
guest, un invité, le convive, un hôte.
to guide, guider.
guilty, coupable.
gun, le fusil ; (=*pistol*) le pistolet ; (*artillery*) le canon.

H

habit, une habitude ; **habitual**, habituel, *f.* -elle.
hair (*of human head*), les cheveux (*m.*) ; (=*of an animal*) le poil ; **I have (get) my hair cut**, je me fais couper les cheveux ; **hairdresser**, le coiffeur, *f.* la coiffeuse.
hale, robuste, sain, bien portant.
half, la moitié ; **half-an-hour**, la demi-heure ; **half dead**, à moitié mort, à demi mort ; **half-open**, entr'ouvert.
hall, la (grande) salle ; (*entrance*) le vestibule ; **Town Hall**, l'hôtel de ville ; (=*mansion*) le château.
ham, le jambon.
hamlet, le hameau.
hammer, le marteau.
hand, la main ; (*of a clock or instrument*) une aiguille ; **in one's hand**, à la main ; **in the hands of (the enemy)**, entre les mains de (l'ennemi) ; **on the other hand**, d'autre part ; **to shake hands with**, serrer la main à, *e.g.* il serra la main au docteur.
to hand over, remettre (mettre).
handbag, le sac à main.

handkerchief, le mouchoir.

handle (*of door*), la poignée ; (*of basket, bucket, etc.*) une anse ; (*of broom*) le manche ; **to handle,** manier.

handsome, beau (bel *before a vowel*), *f.* belle.

to **hang,** pendre (vendre) ; **hanging on the wall,** pendu au mur ; **hanging from the ceiling,** suspendu au plafond.

to **happen,** arriver (*with* être), se passer.

happy, heureux, *f.* -euse ; **I am happy to see you,** je suis heureux de vous voir ; **happily,** heureusement ; **happiness,** le bonheur.

harbour, le port.

hard, dur ; (*blow*) rude ; (=*difficult*) difficile, pénible ; **a hard winter,** un hiver rigoureux ; **to work hard,** travailler dur (ferme) ; **hardness,** la dureté ; **hardly,** à peine.

hare, le lièvre.

harm, le mal ; **to harm,** faire du mal à, *e.g.* mon chien ne vous fera pas de mal ; nuire (*irr.*) à, *e.g.* cela ne leur nuira pas.

to **harness,** atteler.

harsh, dur ; **harshness,** la dureté.

harvest, la moisson.

haste, la hâte, l'empressement (*m.*) ; **in all haste,** en toute hâte.

to **hasten,** se hâter, se dépêcher, se presser, *e.g.* il se hâta (se dépêcha, se pressa, de descendre ; (*with eagerness to please*) s'empresser, *e.g.* le garçon s'empressa de les servir.

hat, le chapeau.

hatchet, la cognée.

hate, hatred, la haine ; **hateful,** odieux ; **to hate,** haïr (*irr.*).

to **have,** avoir ; **to have to (do),** devoir (faire).

hay, le foin.

head, la tête ; **to nod one's head,** hocher la tête ; **to shake one's head,** secouer la tête ; **headmaster,** le directeur ; **headmistress,** la directrice ; **headlamp** (*car*), le phare ; **to fall headlong,** tomber la tête la première ; **to rush headlong,** se précipiter.

to **heal,** guérir (finir).

health, la santé ; **healthy,** sain.

heap, le tas, le monceau.

to **hear,** entendre (vendre) ; **have you heard that he is ill?** avez-vous entendu dire qu'il est malade? **I have heard of you,** j'ai entendu parler de vous ; **a sound was heard,** un bruit se fit entendre ; **have you heard from John?** avez-vous des nouvelles de J.?

heart, le cœur ; **with all my heart,** de tout mon cœur ; **to learn by heart,** apprendre par cœur ; **to laugh heartily,** rire de bon cœur.

hearth, le foyer.

heat, la chaleur.

heath, heather, la bruyère.

heaven, le ciel, *pl.* les cieux.

heavy, lourd.

hedge, la haie.

heel, le talon.

height, la hauteur.

hello! salut !

help, l'aide (*f.*), le secours ; **help!** au secours! **to help,** aider, *e.g.* aidez-moi à monter ; **I can't help laughing,** je ne peux pas m'empêcher de rire.

hen, la poule ; **hen-roost**, le poulailler.
hence, d'ici ; **henceforth**, désormais.
herd, le troupeau.
here, ici ; (*often in conversation*) là ; **here and there**, çà et là ; **here is (are)**, voici, *e.g.* **here they are**, les voici ; **here!** *or* **look here!** tenez!
hero, le héros ; **heroine**, l'héroïne.
to hesitate, hésiter (à) ; **hesitation**, l'hésitation (*f.*).
to hide, cacher ; **to hide oneself**, se cacher ; **he hid his secret from them**, il leur cacha son secret ; **hiding-place**, la cachette.
high, haut ; **higher**, plus haut, supérieur ; **this tower is 20 metres high**, cette tour a 20 mètres de haut.
hill, la colline.
to hire, louer.
history, l'histoire (*f.*).
to hit, frapper ; atteindre (craindre).
to hitch-hike, faire de l'auto-stop.
to hold, tenir (*irr.*) ; **to hold out** (=*extend*), tendre (vendre) ; **to hold back**, retenir ; **to get hold of**, s'emparer de.
hole, le trou.
holiday (*short*), le congé, *e.g.* un jour de congé ; (*long*) les vacances (*f.*) ; (*public*) le jour de fête ; **summer holidays**, les grandes vacances ; **holiday camp**, la colonie de vacances.
Holland, la Hollande.
hollow, creux, *f.* creuse.
holly, le houx.
home, la maison ; **at home**, à la maison, au logis, chez moi (nous, etc.) ; **to come (go, get) home**, rentrer, rentrer à la maison, rentrer chez soi (moi, nous, etc.) ; **make yourself at home**, faites comme chez vous.
homework, les devoirs (*m.*).
honest, honnête ; **an honest fellow**, un brave homme.
honey, le miel.
honour, l'honneur (*m.*) ; **in honour of**, en l'honneur de.
hoof, le sabot.
hope, l'espoir (*m.*) ; (*person's hope*) l'espérance (*f.*), *e.g.* il trompa mes espérances ; **to hope**, espérer, *e.g.* nous espérons réussir.
horse, le cheval, *pl.* -aux ; **horse-shoe**, le fer à cheval ; **horseman**, le cavalier ; **on horseback**, à cheval.
hospital, un hôpital.
host, un hôte, *f.* une hôtesse.
hot, (très) chaud ; **the weather is hot**, il fait (très) chaud ; **I am hot**, j'ai chaud ; **the water is hot**, l'eau est chaude.
hotel, un hôtel ; **hotel-keeper**, un hôtelier.
hour, une heure ; **half-an-hour**, une demi-heure ; **quarter of an hour**, un quart d'heure.
house, la maison ; **to move house**, déménager ; **household**, le ménage ; **housewife**, la ménagère ; **housemaid**, la bonne ; **to do one's housework**, faire son ménage.
how, comment ; **how much (many)**, combien ; **how long**, combien de temps ; **how long have you been waiting?** depuis combien de temps attendez-vous ? **how pretty it is!** comme (*or* que) c'est joli! **how are you?** comment allez-vous ?
however, cependant, pourtant,

toutefois ; **however difficult the problem may be,** si (*or* quelque) difficile que soit le problème.

to howl, hurler.

huge, énorme ; (*in extent*) vaste.

humour, l'humeur (*f.*) ; **in a good humour,** de bonne humeur ; **in a bad humour,** de mauvaise humeur.

hundred, cent ; **one (a) hundred,** cent ; **several (a few) hundred people,** plusieurs (quelques) centaines de personnes.

hunger, la faim ; **hungry,** affamé ; **to be hungry,** avoir faim ; **to be very hungry,** avoir grand'faim, avoir très faim.

hunt(ing), la chasse ; **to hunt,** chasser ; **hunter,** le chasseur.

to hurl, lancer.

to hurry, se dépêcher, se hâter, *e.g.* il se dépêcha (se hâta) de descendre ; **to be in a hurry,** être pressé ; **to hurry along,** presser le pas.

to hurt, faire mal à, *e.g.* cela lui fait mal ; **my dog won't hurt you,** mon chien ne vous fera pas de mal ; **to hurt oneself,** se faire mal.

husband, le mari, l'époux.

hut, la hutte, la cabane.

I

ice, la glace ; **ice-cream,** la glace ; **icy,** glacial.

idea, une idée.

idle, oisif, *f.* oisive ; **idleness,** l'oisiveté (*f.*) ; **to idle about the streets,** flâner dans les rues.

if, si.

to ignore, ignorer.

ill, malade ; **illness,** la maladie ; **to ill-treat,** maltraiter.

to illuminate, éclairer.

to imagine, s'imaginer, se figurer.

to imitate, imiter.

immediately, immédiatement.

immense, immense.

impatient, impatient ; **to get impatient,** s'impatienter ; **impatiently,** avec impatience.

to implore, implorer, supplier.

impolite, impoli.

important, important ; **importance,** l'importance (*f.*).

impossible, impossible ; **impossibility,** l'impossibilité (*f.*).

imprudent, imprudent.

in, dans ; **in there,** là-dedans ; **in front of,** devant.

incessantly, sans cesse.

inclination, une envie ; **to be (feel) inclined to (do),** avoir envie de (faire).

including, y compris, *e.g.* **including wine,** y compris le vin.

incomplete, incomplet, *f.* -ète.

inconvenience, un inconvénient.

to increase, augmenter.

incredible, incroyable.

indeed, en effet.

to indicate, indiquer, désigner.

indifferent, indifférent ; **indifference,** l'indifférence (*f.*).

indispensable, indispensable.

individual, un individu ; (*adj.*) individuel.

indulgent, indulgent.

infant, un petit enfant.

inferior, inférieur.

infinite, infini ; **infinitely,** infiniment.

to inflict, infliger.

to inform, informer, prévenir (venir).

ingenuous, ingénu, naïf, *f.* naïve.
inhabitant, un habitant.
to injure, blesser.
ink, l'encre (*f.*) ; **inkwell, ink-pot**, un encrier.
inn, une auberge ; **inn-keeper**, un aubergiste.
inquisitive, curieux.
inside (*adv.*), dedans, *e.g.* j'ai mis des cailloux dedans ; **to take inside**, faire entrer.
to insist, insister ; **I insist on knowing it**, j'insiste pour le savoir.
to inspect, examiner ; (*luggage*) visitor.
to inspire, inspirer.
instance ; **for instance**, par exemple.
instant, un instant.
instead of, au lieu de ; **instead of working**, au lieu de travailler.
to instruct, instruire (conduire).
instrument, un instrument.
insult, une injure ; **to insult**, insulter.
intelligent, intelligent.
intense, intense.
intention, une intention ; **to intend to (do)**, avoir l'intention de (faire), *e.g.* j'ai l'intention de rester ; **intending to**, dans (avec) l'intention de, *e.g.* dans (avec) l'intention de les surprendre.
interest, l'intérêt (*m.*) ; **to interest**, intéresser ; **to be interested in**, s'intéresser à, *e.g.* il s'intéresse à la littérature ; **interesting**, intéressant.
to interrupt, interrompre (rompre).
to intervene, intervenir (venir).
into, dans.
to introduce (*socially*), présenter.
to invade, envahir (finir) ; **invasion**, une invasion.
to invent, inventer.
to invite, inviter, *e.g.* il m'invita à entrer.
Ireland, l'Irlande (*f.*) ; **Irishman**, un Irlandais ; **Irishwoman**, une Irlandaise.
iron, le fer.
island, une île.
isolated, isolé.
Italy, l'Italie (*f.*) ; **Italian**, un Italien, *f.* une Italienne ; (*language*) l'italien.

J

jacket, le veston.
jam, la confiture *or* les confitures.
janitor, le (la) concierge.
January, janvier (*m.*) ; **in January**, en janvier, au mois de janvier.
jealous, jaloux, *f.* -ouse.
jetty, la jetée.
jewel, le bijou (*pl.* -oux) ; **jewellery**, les bijoux, la bijouterie ; **jeweller**, le bijoutier.
job (=*employment*), un emploi, une place, un poste ; (=*work*) le travail, la besogne.
to join, joindre (craindre) ; **to join** (*people*), rejoindre, *e.g.* il rejoignit ses parents.
to joke, plaisanter ; **joke**, la plaisanterie.
jolly, gai.
to jostle, bousculer.
journey, le voyage, le trajet.
joy, la joie ; **joyful, joyous**, joyeux, *f.* -euse ; **joyfully, joyously**, joyeusement.
jug, le pot, le broc, la cruche.
July, juillet (*m.*) ; **in July**, en juillet, au mois de juillet.
to jump, sauter, bondir (finir).
June, juin (*m.*) ; **in June**, en juin, au mois de juin.

just (*adj.*) juste ; (*adv.*) juste ; **just now,** tout à l'heure ; **he has just gone out,** il vient de sortir ; **he had just gone out,** il venait de sortir ; **just as I was going out,** au moment (à l'instant) où je sortais ; **I am just writing a few letters,** je suis en train d'écrire quelques lettres.

K

keen, vif, *f.* vive.

to **keep,** garder ; (*shop, café, etc.*) tenir (*irr.*) ; **to keep up** (= *maintain*), entretenir ; **to keep (someone) waiting,** faire attendre, *e.g.* il m'a fait attendre.

keeper, (*parks, monuments, etc.*), le gardien ; (= *gamekeeper*) le garde-chasse.

kennel, le chenil, la niche.

key, la clef ; **key-hole,** le trou de la serrure.

to **kill,** tuer.

kilogram, le kilogramme, le kilo (= 2·2 *lbs.*).

kilometre, le kilomètre (= *five eighths of a mile*) ; **we are travelling at 100 kilometres an hour,** nous roulons à cent kilomètres à l'heure.

kind, bon, *f.* bonne ; gentil, *f.* gentille ; aimable ; **kindness,** la bonté ; **kindly** (*adj.*), bienveillant ; **kindly inform us,** veuillez nous informer.

kind (= *sort*), la sorte, une espèce.

king, le roi.

to **kiss,** embrasser ; **kiss** (*noun*), le baiser.

kitchen, la cuisine.

knapsack, le sac.

knee, le genou (*pl.* -x) ; **on one's knees,** à genoux ; **to kneel down,** s'agenouiller.

knife, le couteau ; **penknife,** le canif.

to **knit,** tricoter.

to **knock,** frapper ; **to knock against,** heurter ; **to knock down** (*in accidents, etc.*), renverser ; **to knock over** (*an object*), faire tomber, *e.g.* j'ai fait tomber un joli vase.

to **know,** savoir (*irr.*) ; (= *be acquainted with*) connaître (*irr.*) ; **I know how to drive,** je sais conduire ; **you know French well,** vous connaissez bien le français ; **not to know,** *often expressed by* ignorer, *e.g.* j'ignore la raison de son refus.

knowledge, le savoir, les connaissances (*f.*).

L

lace, la dentelle.

to **lack,** manquer (de), *e.g.* il manque de courage ; **for lack of,** faute de, *e.g.* faute d'argent.

lad, le garçon.

ladder, une échelle.

laden with, chargé de.

lady, la dame ; **young lady,** la demoiselle.

lake, le lac.

lamb, un agneau ; **leg of lamb,** le gigot.

lamp, la lampe ; **street lamp,** le réverbère.

land, la terre ; (= *country*) le pays ; **on land,** à terre ; **to land,** débarquer, aller à terre ; **landing-stage,** le débarcadère.

landing (*in a house*), le palier.

landscape, le paysage.

lane, le petit chemin.

language, la langue ; (=*kind of speech*) le langage.

lap ; on my lap, sur mes genoux.

large, grand ; important.

lash, eye-lash, le cil.

last, dernier, *f.* -ière ; **last year**, l'an dernier ; **last week**, la semaine dernière ; **last night** (=*during the past night*), cette nuit ; (=*yesterday evening*) hier soir ; **at last**, enfin.

to last, durer.

late, tard, *e.g.* il se coucha tard ; (=*after time*) en retard, *e.g.* il arriva en retard.

the latter, celui-ci, *f.* celle-ci.

to laugh, rire (*irr.*) ; **to laugh at**, rire de, se moquer de ; **to laugh heartily**, rire de bon cœur ; **to burst out laughing**, éclater de rire ; **laughter**, le rire ; (=*chorus of laughs*) les rires.

lavatory, la toilette, le cabinet.

lawn, la pelouse.

lawyer, un homme de loi, un avocat.

to lay, poser, mettre (*irr.*) ; **to lay the table**, mettre la table (le couvert).

lazy, paresseux ; **laziness**, la paresse ; **a lazybones**, un paresseux.

to lead, mener, conduire (*irr.*) ; **leader**, le chef.

leaf, la feuille.

league (=4 kms), la lieue.

to lean (*for support*), s'appuyer ; **to lean (over)**, se pencher (sur).

to leap, bondir (finir) ; **leap** (*noun*), le bond.

to learn, apprendre (prendre) ; **to learn to (do)**, apprendre à (faire).

least (*adj.*), le (la) moindre, *e.g.* sans la moindre difficulté ; **least** (*adv.*), le moins, *e.g.* le travail le moins difficile ; **at least**, au moins (*expressing a minimum*), *e.g.* au moins 300 personnes ; du moins (*expressing a reservation*), *e.g.* du moins, je le crois.

leather, le cuir.

leave, le congé, (*military*) la permission ; **to take one's leave**, prendre congé.

to leave (*person or place*), quitter ; (=*start out*) partir (*with* être) ; (=*leave behind*) laisser ; **I left my hat in the train**, j'ai oublié mon chapeau dans le train ; **I have 100 francs left**, il me reste 100 francs.

left (*adj.*), gauche ; **on** (*or* **to**) **the left**, à gauche.

leg, la jambe ; (*of an animal*) la patte.

lemon, le citron.

lemonade, (*still*) la citronnade, (*aerated*) la limonade.

to lend, prêter.

less, moins ; **less than 6 months**, moins de 6 mois ; **I eat less than you**, je mange moins que vous.

lesson, la leçon.

to let (=*allow*), laisser, *e.g.* je les laisse partir ; permettre, *e.g.* je leur permets d'entrer ; **he lets (allows) himself (to) be robbed**, il se laisse voler ; **to let** (*e.g. a house*), louer ; **to let go** (=*loose*), lâcher.

letter, la lettre ; **letter-box**, la boîte aux lettres ; **to post a letter**, mettre une lettre à la poste, jeter une lettre à la boîte.

lettuce, la laitue.
level-crossing, le passage à niveau.
liberty, la liberté.
library, la bibliothèque.
to lick, lécher.
lid, le couvercle.
to lie (*of objects*), se trouver, *e.g.* le village se trouvait au fond d'une vallée ; **to lie down**, se coucher, s'étendre (vendre), s'allonger ; **to lie** (=*be lying*), être couché (étendu, allongé), *e.g.* il était couché au pied d'un arbre.
to lie (=*tell an untruth*), mentir (dormir); **lie**, le mensonge.
life, la vie, l'existence (*f.*) ; **to risk one's life**, risquer la vie ; **never on your life**, jamais de la vie; **life-belt**, la ceinture de sauvetage; **life-boat**, le canot de sauvetage.
to lift, soulever.
lift, un ascenseur.
light, la lumière ; **at first light** (*of day*), au point du jour, au petit jour ; **to put on the light**, allumer (l'électricité) ; **to put (switch) off the light**, couper (éteindre) l'électricité.
to light, allumer ; **to light a fire**, allumer du feu ; **to light up** (=*illumine*), éclairer.
light (*adj.*), (*colour*) clair ; (*weight*) léger ; **it is light** (=*daylight*), il fait jour.
lighthouse, le phare.
lightning, l'éclair (*m.*).
to like, aimer ; **my parents like him**, il plaît à mes parents.
like (=*similar*), semblable, pareil, *f.* pareille ; **to be like**, ressembler à, *e.g.* tu ressembles à ton père ; **what is he like?** comment est-il?
like (*adv.*), comme ; **like that**, comme cela ; **I feel like resting**, j'ai envie de me reposer.
likeable, aimable, sympathique.
likely ; **very likely**, sans doute.
to limp, boiter.
line, la ligne ; (*of cars, etc*) la file ; **to line**, border ; **lined with trees**, bordé d'arbres.
linen (*household, personal*), le linge ; (*material*) la toile.
liner, le paquebot.
to linger, s'attarder.
lining, la doublure.
lion, le lion.
lip, la lèvre.
liquid, le liquide.
list, la liste.
to listen (to), écouter, *e.g.* nous écoutons la musique ; **to listen attentively (to)**, prêter l'oreille (à).
litre, le litre (=$1\frac{3}{4}$ *pints*).
little (*adj.*), petit ; (*adv. of quantity*) peu, *e.g.* peu d'argent; **a little**, un peu ; **little by little**, peu à peu.
to live, vivre (*irr.*) ; (=*dwell*), habiter, demeurer, *e.g.* ils habitent Lyon, ils demeurent à Lyon ; **to live on**, vivre de, *e.g.* ils vivent de pain et de poisson.
living, vivant, en vie ; **to earn one's living**, gagner sa vie.
to load, charger.
loaf, le pain, la miche (de pain).
lock, la serrure ; **to lock**, fermer à clef ; **to lock in**, enfermer à clef.
lodge (*porter's, etc.*), la loge.
loft, le grenier.
London, Londres.
lonely, solitaire ; (=*isolated*) isolé.

long (*adj.*), long, *f.* longue ; **this room is 5 metres long,** cette pièce a 5 mètres de long ; **a long time,** longtemps ; **longer** (*time*), plus longtemps ; **how long?** combien de temps? **no longer,** ne . . . plus ; **as long as,** tant que, *e.g.* tant que je vivrai ; **to be long (doing),** tarder à (faire), *e.g.* il ne tarda pas à revenir.

to look (at), regarder ; **to look out of,** regarder par, *e.g.* elle regardait par la fenêtre ; **to look round,** se retourner ; **to look up,** lever la tête (*or* les yeux) ; **to look away,** détourner la tête (les yeux) ; **to look for,** chercher ; **to look after** (*medically*), soigner ; **to look out upon,** donner sur, *e.g.* ma chambre donne sur la cour ; **to look** (=*appear*), paraître, avoir l'air, *e.g.* tu parais fatigué, tu as l'air fatigué ; **to look like,** avoir l'air de, *e.g.* il a l'air d'un gorille ; **to look well** (*in health*), avoir bonne mine ; **look out!** attention!

look (*noun*), le regard.

looking-glass, le miroir, la glace.

to loose, lâcher.

lord, le seigneur.

to lose, perdre (vendre) ; (=*mislay*) égarer.

loss, la perte.

lost, perdu ; **to get lost** (= *having strayed*), s'égarer.

lot (=*fate*), le sort.

a lot (of), beaucoup (de) ; **what a lot of . . .!** que de . . . !

loud, fort ; **louder,** plus fort ; **loudly,** fort.

lounge (*room*), le salon.

love, l'amour (*m.*); **to love,** aimer.

lovely, admirable, superbe, splendide.

low, bas, *f.* basse ; **lower,** plus bas, inférieur.

luck, le bonheur, la chance ; **luckily,** par bonheur, heureusement ; **to be lucky,** avoir de la chance.

luggage, les bagages (*m.*) ; **luggage-room,** la consigne ; **luggage-rack** (*train*), le filet.

luke-warm, tiède.

lunch, le déjeuner ; **to have lunch,** déjeuner.

lying, couché, étendu.

M

machine-gun, la mitrailleuse ; **sub-machine-gun,** la mitraillette.

mad, fou, *f.* folle ; **madly,** follement ; **madness,** la folie.

madam, madame, *pl.* mesdames.

magazine, le magazine, la revue.

magnificent, magnifique.

maid (*servant*), la bonne, la femme de chambre.

mail, le courrier.

main, principal ; **main road,** la route.

to maintain, entretenir (tenir).

to make, faire (*irr.*) ; **to make** (+*adj.*), rendre (vendre), *e.g.* cela me rend malade ; **he makes himself respected,** il se fait respecter ; **to make for** (=*go towards*), se diriger vers ; **to make out,** distinguer; **to make up** (*with cosmetics*), se maquiller; **make-up,** le maquillage.

man, un homme; **old man,** le vieillard.

to manage to (do), arriver à (faire), parvenir à (faire).

manager, le directeur ; (*café,*

hotel) le gérant.
manner, la manière; **the manner in which** (he plays), la manière dont (il joue).
mansion (*country*), le château.
mantelpiece, la cheminée.
manufacturer, le fabricant.
many, beaucoup ; **how many**, combien ; **too many**, trop ; **so many**, tant ; **as many**, autant.
marble, le marbre; (*toy*) la bille.
March, mars (*m.*) ; **in March**, en mars, au mois de mars.
mare, la jument.
margin, la marge.
mark, la marque; (*work*) la note.
market, le marché ; **market-place**, la place du marché.
marriage, le mariage.
to **marry**, épouser, se marier avec, *e.g.* elle a épousé un Américain, elle s'est mariée avec un Américain.
marvel, la merveille ; **marvellous**, merveilleux.
mason, le maçon.
mass (*church*), la messe ; **high mass**, la grand'messe.
master, le maître ; (*school*) le professeur.
match, une allumette ; (*game*) la partie, le match.
material (=*stuff*), une étoffe.
mathematics, les mathématiques (*f.*).
matter ; **what is the matter?** qu'y a-t-il ? **what is the matter with him?** qu'a-t-il ? qu'est-ce qu'il a ? **it is a matter (question) of**, il s'agit de, *e.g.* il s'agit de trouver la clef ; **that does not matter**, cela ne fait rien ; **no matter**, n'importe ; **as a matter of fact**, à vrai dire.
May, mai (*m.*) ; **in May**, en mai, au mois de mai.
may I (do)? puis-je (faire)?
mayor, le maire.
meadow, la prairie, le pré.
meal, le repas.
mean, avare.
to **mean**, vouloir dire, *e.g.* que voulez-vous dire ? signifier, *e.g.* que signifie ce mot ?
means, le moyen, les moyens ; **by means of**, au moyen de.
meanwhile, pendant ce temps.
to **measure**, mesurer.
meat, la viande.
Mediterranean, la Méditerranée ; (*adj.*) méditerranéen, *f.* -enne.
to **meet**, rencontrer ; **they have met in Paris**, ils se sont rencontrés à Paris ; **the committee meets**, le comité se réunit (réunir, *like* finir).
meeting (=*encounter*), la rencontre ; **he went to meet them**, il alla à leur rencontre.
melancholy, la mélancolie ; (*adj.*) mélancolique.
to **melt**, fondre (vendre).
memory, la mémoire ; (=*something remembered*) le souvenir.
to **mend** (*clothes, etc.*), raccommoder.
to **mention**, mentionner, parler de ; **don't mention it!** il n'y a pas de quoi!
menu, le menu.
merchandise, la marchandise.
merchant, le marchand.
merely, seulement, ne . . . que ; **he merely smiled**, il se contenta de sourire, il ne fit que sourire.
merry, joyeux, *f.* -euse ; **merrily**, joyeusement.

message, le message; **messenger,** le messager.

metal, le métal.

method, la méthode.

metre, le mètre.

middle, le milieu; **in the middle of,** au milieu de.

midnight, minuit.

might (=*strength*), la force, les forces; **with all my might,** de toutes mes forces.

mighty, puissant.

mild, doux, *f.* douce.

mile, le mille; **5 miles,** 5 milles.

milk, le lait.

mill, le moulin; **windmill,** le moulin à vent; **miller,** le meunier.

mind, l'esprit (*m.*); **to make up one's mind to (do),** se décider à (faire); **to mind** (=*look after*), garder; **I don't mind,** cela m'est égal; **mind your own business,** mêlez-vous de ce qui vous regarde; **never mind!** n'importe!

mine, le mien, etc; **this hat is mine,** ce chapeau est à moi; **a friend of mine,** un de mes amis; **a doctor friend of mine,** un médecin de mes amis.

to **mingle,** mêler; **he mingled with the crowd,** il se mêla à la foule.

minute, la minute.

mirror, le miroir, la glace.

miser, un avare; **miserly,** avare.

misfortune, le malheur.

to **mislay,** égarer.

Miss, mademoiselle, *pl.* mesdemoiselles.

to **miss,** manquer; **he just missed falling,** il faillit tomber.

mist, la brume, le brouillard; **it is misty,** il fait du brouillard.

mistake, la faute; **to make a mistake, to be mistaken,** se tromper; **to mistake** (*one thing for another*), se tromper de, *e.g.* je me suis trompé de numéro.

mistress, la maîtresse.

misunderstanding, le malentendu.

to **mix,** mêler, mélanger; **he mixed with the crowd,** il se mêla à la foule; **to mix up** (=*confuse*), confondre (vendre).

to **moan,** gémir (finir); **moan,** le gémissement.

to **mock** (at), se moquer (de), *e.g.* ils se moquèrent de nous.

modern, moderne.

moist, humide.

moment, un moment, un instant; **a moment after,** un moment (instant) après; **the moment after,** le moment (l'instant) d'après; **at the moment when,** au moment (à l'instant) où; **for the moment,** pour le moment (l'instant).

Monday, lundi (*m.*); **last Monday,** lundi dernier; **next Monday,** lundi prochain.

money, l'argent (*m.*); **ready money, cash,** l'argent comptant.

monkey, le singe.

month, le mois; **every month,** tous les mois; **next month,** le mois prochain; **last month,** le mois dernier.

monument, le monument.

moon, la lune; **moonlight,** le clair de lune.

to **moor,** amarrer; **mooring-rope,** une amarre.

more, plus; **more than** (*a quantity*), plus de, *e.g.* plus de 1000 francs; **you eat more**

than I, vous mangez plus que moi ; **more and more,** de plus en plus ; **no more, not any more,** ne . . . plus ; **some more bread,** encore du pain ; **more** (*in comparisons*), davantage, *e.g.* j'ai beaucoup de livres, mais vous en avez davantage.

moreover, d'ailleurs, de plus.

morning, le matin ; (*as in " a busy morning ", etc.*) la matinée ; **good morning!** bonjour! **Sunday morning,** dimanche matin ; **from morning till night,** du matin au soir ; **early in the morning,** de bon matin, de grand matin ; le matin, de bonne heure.

morrow, le lendemain.

mosquito, le moustique.

most, le plus, *e.g.* le plus important ; le plus d'argent ; **the most charming man,** l'homme le plus charmant ; **a most charming man,** un homme des plus charmants ; **most** (=*majority*), la plupart, *e.g.* la plupart des hommes ; (= *greater portion*) la plus grande partie, *e.g.* il avait dépensé la plus grande partie de sa fortune.

moth, le papillon de nuit.

mother, la mère; (*fam.*) maman; **mother-in-law,** la belle-mère.

motionless, immobile.

motive, le motif.

motor-car, une auto(mobile), la voiture ; **motor coach,** un autocar, un car.

mountain, la montagne ; **mountainous,** montagneux.

mouse, la souris.

mouth, la bouche ; (*of an animal*) la gueule ; (*of a river*) une embouchure ; **mouthful,** la bouchée.

to **move** (*intrans.*), bouger ; (*trans.*) remuer ; **to move (walk) away,** s'éloigner ; **to move (go) back,** reculer ; **to move aside,** (s') écarter ; **to move house,** déménager ; **moved** (*emotionally*), ému ; **movement,** le mouvement.

much, beaucoup (de) ; **how much,** combien ; **too much,** trop ; **so much,** tant ; **as much,** autant.

mud, la boue ; **muddy,** boueux.

muffled, sourd.

multitude, la multitude.

to **munch** (*e.g. an apple*), croquer.

to **murmur,** murmurer.

mushroom, le champignon.

music, la musique ; **musician,** le musicien, *f.* la musicienne.

must, *expressed by* devoir, *e.g.* **he must go out,** il doit sortir ; **he must have gone out,** il a dû sortir.

mustard, la moutarde.

mute, muet, *f.* muette.

N

nail, le clou, *pl.* les clous.

naked, nu.

name, le nom ; **what is your name?** quel est votre nom? *or* comment vous appelez-vous? **my name is John,** mon nom est Jean *or* je m'appelle Jean ; **to name,** nommer.

nap, le somme ; **to have (take) a nap,** faire un somme.

narrow, étroit.

nasty, mauvais, vilain ; **a nasty trick,** un vilain tour.

nation, la nation ; **national,**

national; **nationality**, la nationalité.

native (=*of one's birth*), natal, *e.g.* mon pays natal; **native** (=*born in*) originaire, *e.g.* il était originaire de Marseille; **native** (*coloured, aborigine*), un (une) indigène.

natural, naturel, *f.* -elle; **naturally**, naturellement.

nature, la nature.

near (*adj.*), proche; **near** (*prep.*), près (de); **to draw near (to)**, s'approcher (de); **quite near (to)**, tout près (de); **nearly**, presque, à peu près; **nearly 3 o'clock**, près de 3 heures; **he nearly fell**, il faillit tomber.

necessary, nécessaire; **it is necessary to wait**, il est nécessaire d'attendre, il faut attendre.

neck, le cou; **he threw his arms round his mother's neck**, il se jeta au cou de sa mère.

necklace, le collier.

need, le besoin; **to have need of, to need**, avoir besoin de.

needle, une aiguille.

to **neglect**, négliger; **negligence, neglect**, la négligence; **negligent**, négligent.

negro, le nègre, *f.* la négresse.

to **neigh**, hennir (finir); **neigh (ing)**, le hennissement.

neighbour, le voisin, *f.* la voisine; **neighbouring**, voisin; **neighbourhood**, le voisinage.

neither . . . nor, ne . . . ni . . . ni, *e.g.* **he has neither relatives nor friends**, il n'a ni parents ni amis; **neither is speaking the truth**, ni l'un ni l'autre ne dit la vérité; **John won't come.—Neither shall I.** Jean ne viendra pas.—Ni moi non plus.

nephew, le neveu.

nerve, le nerf.

nest, le nid.

net, le filet.

never, ne . . . jamais; (*used alone*) jamais; **never on your life**, jamais de la vie; **never mind**, n'importe.

nevertheless, néanmoins.

new (=*just bought*), neuf, *f.* neuve; (=*fresh*) nouveau (nouvel *before a vowel*), *f.* nouvelle; **the New Year**, le nouvel an; **New Year's Day**, le jour de l'an; **New Year's gift**, les étrennes (*f.*); **a happy New Year!** bonne année!

newcomer, le nouveau-venu, la nouvelle-venue.

news, les nouvelles (*f.*); **piece of news**, la nouvelle; **have you any news of John?** avez-vous des nouvelles de Jean?; **news** (*broadcast*), les informations (*f.*).

newspaper, le journal (*pl.* -aux).

New Zealand, la Nouvelle-Zélande: **New-Zealander**, le (la) Néo-Zélandais(e).

next (*adv.*), puis; **next** (*adj.*), prochain, *e.g.* la semaine prochaine, le mois prochain; **next Monday**, lundi prochain; **next day**, le lendemain; **next morning**, le lendemain matin; **next to**, à côté de, *e.g.* il s'assit à côté de moi; **next door**, à côté, *e.g.* ils habitent à côté.

nice (*of persons*), aimable, gentil, *f.* gentille; (*of things*) joli.

niece, la nièce.

night, la nuit; **night and day**, nuit et jour; **from morning**

till night, du matin au soir ; **at nightfall,** à la nuit tombante, à la tombée de la nuit ; **good night!** bonne nuit! **last night** (=*yesterday evening*), hier soir ; **I haven't slept a wink all night,** je n'ai pas fermé l'œil de la nuit.

nightingale, le rossignol.

nobleman, le gentilhomme, *pl.* les gentilshommes.

nobody, ne . . . personne ; (*used alone*) personne ; **nobody else,** personne d'autre.

to **nod the head,** hocher la tête.

noise, le bruit ; **noisy,** bruyant ; **noisily,** bruyamment, à grand bruit.

noon, midi.

nor, ni ; **nor I (either),** ni moi non plus.

Normandy, la Normandie.

north, le nord.

nose, le nez ; **to blow one's nose,** se moucher.

note (*bank*), le billet ; **100 franc note,** le billet de cent francs ; (=*short letter*) le billet.

to **note** (=*notice*), remarquer.

note-book, le carnet.

nothing, ne . . . rien ; (*used alone*) rien ; **I say nothing,** je ne dis rien ; je me tais ; **I have nothing to do,** je n'ai rien à faire.

to **notice,** remarquer, apercevoir ; (*a fact*) s'apercevoir, *e.g.* je m'aperçus qu'il tremblait.

notice, un avis ; **notice-board** (*House for Sale, etc.*), un écriteau.

novel, le roman.

November, novembre ; **in November,** en novembre, au mois de novembre.

now, maintenant ; (*beginning a fresh paragraph*) or ; (*stressed*) à présent, *e.g.* **what is he doing** *now*? que fait-il à présent? **just now,** tout à l'heure ; **up till now,** jusqu'ici, jusqu'à présent ; **he is certainly back by now,** il est certainement de retour à cette heure.

nowhere, ne . . . nulle part, *e.g.* je n'ai vu cela nulle part.

number, le nombre ; (*in a series*) le numéro, *e.g.* le numéro de votre maison.

numerous, nombreux.

nun, la religieuse.

nurse, la garde-malade, une infirmière.

O

oak(-tree), le chêne.

obedience, l'obéissance (*f.*).

to **obey,** obéir (finir), *e.g.* **I obey him,** je lui obéis.

object, un objet.

objection, une objection.

to **oblige,** obliger, *e.g.* il m'obligea à payer ; je suis obligé de payer.

to **observe,** observer ; **observation,** une observation.

to **obtain,** obtenir (tenir).

obvious, évident ; **obviously,** évidemment.

occasionally, parfois, de temps à autre.

occupation, une occupation, le métier.

to **occupy,** occuper.

to **occur** (=*happen*), arriver (*with* être) ; **the idea occurred to me that . . . ,** l'idée me vint que . . . ; **it occurred to me that . . . ,** il me vint à l'esprit (à l'idée) que. . . .

ocean, un océan.
October, octobre (*m.*) ; **in October**, en octobre, au mois d'octobre.
odious, odieux.
of course, bien entendu, naturellement.
to offer, offrir (ouvrir), *e.g.* je lui offris de l'aider ; (=*hold out*) tendre (vendre).
office, le bureau.
officer, un officier.
often, souvent.
old, vieux (vieil *before a vowel*), *f.* vieille ; (=*former*) ancien, *f.* ancienne ; **old man**, le vieillard ; **old fellow (chap)**, le bonhomme ; **old age**, la vieillesse ; **to grow old**, vieillir (finir) ; **how old are you?** quel âge avez-vous? **in the old days**, autrefois, jadis.
omelet, une omelette.
to omit, omettre (mettre).
on, on to, sur ; **on a cold night**, par une nuit froide.
once, une fois ; **once more**, encore une fois ; **at once**, tout de suite, à l'instant.
onion, un oignon.
only (*adj.*), seul ; **one and only**, unique, *e.g.* son fils unique ; **only** (*adv.*), seulement, ne . . . que ; **not only**, non seulement.
to open, ouvrir (*irr.*) ; **the door opens**, la porte s'ouvre ; **open(ed)** ouvert ; **half-open**, entr'ouvert ; **open-mouthed**, bouche bée ; **in the open country (sea)**, en pleine campagne (mer) ; **to sleep in the open**, coucher à la belle étoile.
opinion, un avis ; **in my opinion**, à mon avis.
opportunity, une occasion.
opposite (*adj.*), opposé, *e.g.* le côté opposé ; (*prep.*) en face de, *e.g.* en face de l'église ; **the house opposite**, la maison d'en face.
or, ou ; **or else**, ou bien.
orange, une orange.
orchard, le verger.
orchestra, un orchestre.
order, un ordre ; (*shop, business*) la commande ; **in order that**, pour que *or* afin que +*subj.*, *e.g.* pour qu'il puisse venir, afin qu'il puisse venir.
to order, ordonner, commander, *e.g.* je leur ordonne (commande) de sortir.
ordinary, ordinaire.
other, autre ; **otherwise**, autrement ; **they know each other**, ils se connaissent.
ought, *expressed by* devoir, *e.g.* **you ought to do it**, vous devriez le faire ; **you ought to have done it**, vous auriez dû le faire.
out, hors de, *e.g.* il se précipita hors de la maison ; **out of politeness**, par politesse ; **he took a key out of his pocket**, il prit une clef dans sa poche, *or* il tira une clef de sa poche, *or* il sortit une clef de sa poche ; **he jumped out of bed**, il sauta à bas de son lit ; **he was reading out of a big book**, il lisait dans un gros livre ; **out of the way** (=*apart*), à l'écart, *e.g.* il restait à l'écart ; **nine out of ten**, neuf sur dix ; **to go (come) out**, sortir (*with* être) ; **to put out** (=*extinguish*), éteindre (craindre) ; **to go out** (=*be extinguished*), s'éteindre, *e.g.* le feu s'éteint ; **to set out** (=*depart*), partir (*with* être) ;

to **hold out** (=*extend*), tendre (vendre); **to look out of**, regarder par, *e.g.* elle regardait par la fenêtre; **to make out** (=*distinguish*), distinguer; **I can't make it out** (=*I can't understand it*), je n'y comprends rien.

to **outlive**, survivre à, *e.g.* elle survécut à son mari.

outset, le commencement; (*of a career, etc.*) le début.

outside (*adv.*), dehors; (*prep.*) en dehors de.

oven, le four.

over (*prep.*), sur; (=*above*) au-dessus de, *e.g.* au-dessus de nos têtes; (*motion over*) par-dessus, *e.g.* il sauta par-dessus le mur; **she wears an apron over her dress**, elle porte un tablier par-dessus sa robe; **over there**, là-bas; **to pass over**, franchir (finir); **to hand over**, remettre (mettre); **to watch over**, surveiller.

over (=*finished*), terminé, fini.

overall (*coat*), la blouse.

overcoat (*man's*), le pardessus; (*woman's*) le manteau.

overcome with (fatigue), accablé de (fatigue).

to **overflow**, déborder.

to **overhear**, surprendre (prendre).

to **overlook**, donner sur, *e.g.* ma chambre donne sur la cour; (=*rise above*) dominer, *e.g.* le château domine la ville.

to **overtake**, rattraper.

to **overturn**, renverser.

to **overwhelm**, accabler.

to **owe**, devoir (*irr.*).

owl, le hibou (*pl.* -x).

own, propre, *e.g.* mes propres mains.

to **own**, posséder.

owner, le (la) propriétaire.

ox, le bœuf.

oyster, une huître.

P

pace (=*step*), le pas.

package, packet, le paquet.

pail, le seau.

pain, la douleur; **painful**, (*physical*) douloureux, (*moral*) pénible.

to **paint**, peindre (craindre); **painter** (*artist*), le peintre; (*buildings*) le peintre en bâtiments; **paint** (*material*), la peinture.

pair, la paire.

pal, le copain, la copine.

palace, le palais.

pale, pâle; **to go (grow) pale**, pâlir (finir).

pane, la vitre, le carreau.

paper, le papier; **blotting-paper**, le (papier) buvard.

paraffin, le pétrole.

parcel, le paquet, le colis.

to **pardon**, pardonner, *e.g.* je lui pardonne sa faute; **I beg your pardon** (*apology*), je vous demande pardon; **(I beg your) pardon?** plaît-il? pardon?

parents, les parents (*m.*).

parish, la paroisse; **parishioner**, le paroissien; **parish priest**, le curé.

Parisian, le Parisien, *f.* la Parisienne.

park, le parc; le jardin public; **park-keeper**, le gardien.

to **park**, stationner.

parrot, le perroquet.

part, la partie; **to be a part of**, faire partie de, *e.g.* la Conciergerie fait partie du Palais de Justice ; **part** (*in a play*), le rôle ; **to take part in,** prendre part à.

to part (=*separate*), se séparer, *e.g.* ils se séparèrent à minuit.

particular, particulier ; **particularly,** particulièrement.

party (=*group of people*), la compagnie, la société ; (= *social gathering*) la réunion, la soirée.

to pass, passer (*with* avoir *or* être) ; **I pass the church,** je passe devant l'église ; **I pass the wood,** je passe près du bois (à côté du bois, le long du bois) ; **to pass** (=*go beyond*), dépasser ; **to pass** (*going in opposite directions*), croiser, *e.g.* je les ai croisés dans la rue ; **to pass through,** traverser.

passage, le couloir.

passenger (*train, bus*), le voyageur ; (*ship, plane*) le passager ; **passenger-ship,** le paquebot.

passer-by, le passant.

passport, le passeport.

past, le passé ; **as in the past,** comme par le passé ; **past** (*adj.*), passé.

pastry, la pâtisserie ; **pastry-cook,** le pâtissier ; **pastry-cook's shop, confectionery,** la pâtisserie.

path, le sentier ; (*in park, etc.*) une allée.

patient, patient ; **patience,** la patience ; **to lose patience,** perdre patience.

patient (*doctor's*), le (la) malade ; le client, *f.* la cliente.

pavement, le trottoir.

paw, la patte.

to pay, payer, *e.g.* j'ai payé les billets ; **to pay attention,** faire attention.

pay (*professions, etc.*), le traitement ; (*workman's*) le salaire.

peace, la paix ; **peaceful,** paisible ; **peacefulness,** la paix, la tranquillité.

peach, la pêche ; **peach-tree,** le pêcher.

peak (*mountain*), la cime.

pear, la poire ; **pear-tree,** le poirier.

peas, les petits pois.

peasant, le paysan, *f.* la paysanne.

pebble, le caillou (*pl.* -x).

peculiar, particulier.

pedestrian, le piéton.

pen, le porte-plume ; **pen-nib,** le bec de plume ; **fountain-pen,** le stylo.

pencil, le crayon.

to penetrate, pénétrer.

penknife, le canif.

people, les gens ; **a lot of people,** beaucoup de gens, beaucoup de monde ; **several people,** plusieurs personnes ; **French people,** les Français ; **other people,** les autres, les autres gens ; **people** (*of a country*), le peuple, *e.g.* le peuple anglais.

pepper, le poivre.

to perceive, apercevoir (recevoir).

perch (*fish*), la perche.

to perch (*birds*) ; se percher.

perfect, parfait ; **perfectly,** parfaitement.

to perform (*theatre*), jouer, représenter ; **performance,** la représentation.

perfume, le parfum ; **to perfume,** parfumer.

perhaps, peut-être ; **perhaps you**

are right, peut-être avez-vous raison.

period, une époque.

to perish, périr (finir).

to permit, permettre (mettre), *e.g.* je lui permets de le faire; **permission (to)**, la permission (de).

perplexed, perplexe, embarrassé.

person, la personne; **personal**, personnel; **personnel**, le personnel.

to perspire, transpirer.

to persuade, persuader.

petrol, l'essence (*f.*); **petrol pump**, le poste d'essence.

pharmacy, la pharmacie.

pheasant, le faisan.

photograph, la photographie; **photographer**, le photographe; **to photograph**, photographier.

piano, le piano.

to pick (=*gather*), cueillir (*irr.*); **to pick up**, ramasser.

picnic, le pique-nique; **to picnic**, faire (un) pique-nique, piqueniquer.

picture, une image; (*artist's*) le tableau.

picturesque, pittoresque.

piece, le morceau; (*coin*) la pièce, *e.g.* une pièce de 5 fr.

pier, la jetée.

to pierce, percer.

pig, le cochon, le porc.

pigeon, le pigeon.

pile, le tas.

pill, la pilule.

pin, une épingle.

pine (-tree), le pin.

pink, rose.

pipe, la pipe; **to fill a pipe**, bourrer une pipe.

pity, la pitié; **to take pity on**, avoir pitié de; **pitiful**, **piteous**, pitoyable, piteux; **what a pity!** quel dommage! **it is a pity that**, c'est dommage que +*subj.*; **to pity**, plaindre (craindre).

place, un endroit, le lieu; **in place of**, à la place de; **in your place**, à votre place; **to take place**, avoir lieu.

to place, placer, mettre, poser.

plain, la plaine.

plain (*adj.*), simple; (=*clear*) clair.

plan, le projet, le plan.

plane, un aéroplane, un avion; **by plane**, en avion.

plane (-tree), le platane.

plank, la planche.

plant, la plante; **to plant**, planter.

plate, une assiette.

platform (*station*), le quai, le trottoir.

to play, jouer; **to play tennis (football,** *etc.*), jouer au tennis (au football, etc.); **to play the piano (violin** *etc.*), jouer du piano (du violon, *etc.*); **to play** (=*perform in theatre*), jouer, représenter; **to play about**, gambader.

play (*noun*), le jeu, *pl.* les jeux; (*theatre*) la pièce de théâtre.

player, le joueur.

playground, la cour (de récréation).

plaything, le jouet, le joujou (*pl.* -x).

playtime, la récréation.

pleasant, agréable; (*person*) aimable.

to please, plaire (*irr.*), *e.g.* vous plaisez à mes parents; **that pleases us**, cela nous plaît, *or* cela nous fait plaisir; **if you**

please, s'il vous (te) plaît ; **don't do that, please!** ne faites pas cela, je vous en prie!
pleased, content, *e.g.* je suis content de vous voir ; **I shall be only too pleased**, je ne demande pas mieux.
pleasure, le plaisir ; **with pleasure**, avec plaisir.
plenty (of), beaucoup (de).
plough, la charrue ; **to plough**, labourer ; **ploughman**, le laboureur.
to pluck (=*gather*), cueillir (*irr.*).
pluck (=*courage*), le courage.
plum, la prune ; **plum-tree**, le prunier.
poacher, le braconnier.
pocket, la poche ; **pocket-money**, l'argent de poche.
poem, le poème.
point, le point ; **to be on the point of (doing)**, être sur le point de (faire), *e.g.* j'étais sur le point de protester, *or* j'allais protester.
to point to, indiquer, désigner.
police, la police ; **policeman**, **police constable**, (*town*) l'agent de police, (*country*) le gendarme ; **police station**, le poste de police, la gendarmerie ; **superintendent of police**, le commissaire de police.
to polish (*shoes*), cirer.
polite poli ; **politely**, poliment ; **politeness**, la politesse.
pond (*natural*), la mare, un étang ; (*ornamental*) le bassin.
pool, un étang.
poor, pauvre ; **poorly**, pauvrement.
poplar, le peuplier.
pork, le porc ; **pork-butcher**, le charcutier.
port, le port ; **sea-port**, le port de mer.
porter (*railway*), un employé ; (*luggage*) le porteur ; (*of building*) le (la) concierge, le portier.
portion, la partie.
position, la position.
to possess, posséder.
possession, la possession ; **to get possession of**, s'emparer de.
possible, possible ; **possibility**, la possibilité.
post (=*job*), le poste, la place.
post (*mail*), la poste ; **post-office** (*main*), l'hôtel des postes, (*small*) le bureau de poste ; **postman**, le facteur ; **postcard**, la carte postale ; **postage-stamp**, le timbre-poste, *pl.* les timbres-poste ; **post box**, la boîte aux lettres ; **to post a letter**, mettre une lettre à la poste, jeter une lettre à la boîte.
poster, une affiche.
pot, le pot.
potato, la pomme de terre, *pl.* les pommes de terre.
poultry, la volaille ; **poultry-yard**, la basse-cour.
pound, la livre.
to pour (out), verser.
poverty, la pauvreté, la misère.
powder, la poudre ; **to powder**, poudrer.
power, le pouvoir, la puissance ; **powerful**, puissant.
prayer, la prière.
to precede, précéder ; **preceding**, précédent.
precious, précieux.
precise, précis ; **precisely**, précisément, justement.
to prefer, préférer, aimer mieux,

e.g. je préfère attendre, j'aime mieux attendre.

preparation, le préparatif ; (*school*) les devoirs (*m.*) ; **preparation-room,** la salle d'étude.

to prepare, préparer ; **to prepare to (do),** se préparer (*or* se disposer, *or* s'apprêter) à (faire).

presence, la présence.

to present, présenter.

present (*adj.*), présent, actuel, *f.* actuelle ; **at present,** à présent, en ce moment, à l'heure qu'il est ; **to be present at,** assister à, *e.g.* j'ai assisté à la première représentation.

present (=*gift*), le cadeau ; **New Year's present,** les étrennes (*f.*).

presently, tout à l'heure, dans un instant.

to preserve, conserver.

president, le président.

to press, presser.

to pretend, faire semblant de, *e.g.* il faisait semblant de dormir ; feindre (craindre), *e.g.* il feignit de me croire.

prettily, gentiment.

pretty, joli.

to prevent, empêcher, *e.g.* je les empêcherai de sortir ; je les en empêcherai.

previous, précédent, *e.g.* la semaine précédente.

price, le prix ; **at any price,** à tout prix.

to prick, piquer.

pride (*legitimate*), la fierté ; (*arrogant*) l'orgueil (*m.*).

priest, le prêtre ; **parish priest,** le curé ; **priest's house,** le presbytère.

prince, le prince ; **princess,** la princesse.

principal (=*director*), le principal, le directeur.

principal (*adj.*), principal.

to print, imprimer.

prison, la prison ; **prisoner,** le prisonnier.

private, privé, particulier.

probable, probable ; **probably,** probablement.

problem, le problème.

procession, le cortège.

to procure, se procurer.

to produce, produire (conduire).

professor, le professeur.

to profit (by), profiter (de).

progress, les progrès (*m.*) ; **to make progress,** faire des progrès.

project, le projet.

to prolong, prolonger.

promise, la promesse ; **I keep my promise,** je tiens ma promesse ; **to promise,** promettre (mettre), *e.g.* je lui ai promis de l'aider.

prompt, prompt ; **promptly,** promptement.

to pronounce, prononcer.

proof, la preuve.

proposal, la proposition ; (*of marriage*) la demande en mariage.

to propose, proposer, *e.g.* je lui propose de l'accompagner.

proprietor, le propriétaire ; **proprietress,** la propriétaire.

to protect, protéger.

proud (*rightly*), fier, *f.* fière ; **proudly,** fièrement ; **proud** (=*arrogant*), orgueilleux.

to prove, prouver.

to provide, fournir (finir).

providing (provided) that, pourvu que +*subj.*

province, la province.

to prowl, rôder.
prudent, prudent ; **prudence**, la prudence.
public, public, *f.* publique.
to pull, tirer, traîner ; **to pull down** (*buildings*), démolir (finir).
pullover, le pullover.
punch, le coup de poing ; **I punched him**, je lui ai donné un coup de poing.
punctual, ponctuel, exact.
to punish, punir (finir) ; **punishment**, la punition, le châtiment.
pupil, un(e) élève.
to purchase, acheter; **purchase**, un achat, une emplette.
pure, pur.
purpose, le dessein ; **on purpose, purposely**, à dessein, exprès.
purse, le porte-monnaie ; la bourse.
to pursue, poursuivre (suivre).
to push, pousser ; **to push back** (away), repousser ; **to push about** (*roughly*), bousculer.
to put, mettre (*irr.*), poser ; **to put on**, mettre ; **to put down**, déposer ; **to put aside**, mettre de côté ; **to put back**, remettre ; **to put out** (=*extinguish*), éteindre (craindre).
pyjamas, le pyjama.

Q

quadrangle, la cour.
quality, la qualité.
quantity, la quantité.
quarrel, la querelle, la dispute ; **quarrelsome**, querelleur ; **to quarrel**, se quereller, se disputer.
quarter (*fraction*), le quart ; **quarter of an hour**, le quart d'heure ; (*of a town*) le quartier.
quay, le quai.
queen, la reine ; (*cards*) la dame.
queer, drôle.
question, la question ; **to ask a question**, poser une question ; **it is a question of**, il est question de, *or* il s'agit de, *e.g.* il s'agit de trouver la clef ; **to question**, questionner, interroger.
quick (*adj.*), rapide ; vif, *f.* vive ; **quick to** (do), prompt à (faire) ; **quickly**, vite, rapidement, vivement ; **to quicken one's step** (pace), presser le pas.
quiet, calme, tranquille ; (= *silent*) silencieux ; **quietly**, doucement, tranquillement ; **to speak quietly**, parler (tout) bas, parler à voix basse ; **quietness**, la tranquillité, (=*silence*) le silence.
quite, tout à fait ; **there were quite 200 people**, il y avait bien 200 personnes.

R

rabbit, le lapin.
radiator, le radiateur.
radio, la radio, la T.S.F.
radish, le radis.
raft, le radeau.
rage, la colère ; **to get into a rage**, se mettre en colère.
rags, les haillons (*m.*), les guenilles (*f.*) ; **in rags (tatters)** en haillons, déguenillé.
rail, le rail ; **by rail**, en chemin de fer ; par le train.
railway, le chemin de fer ; **railway line**, la ligne de chemin de fer ; **railway track**, la voie ferrée.

rain, la pluie ; **to rain**, pleuvoir ; **it rains** *or* **it is raining**, il pleut ; **it was raining**, il pleuvait ; **it had rained** *or* **it had been raining**, il avait plu ; **it rains in torrents**, il pleut à verse ; **rainy**, pluvieux ; **rain-coat**, un imperméable.

to raise, lever ; **to raise** (*high*), élever ; **to raise** (=*breed* *or* *rear*), élever.

rake, le râteau ; **to rake**, râtisser.

at random, au hasard.

rank, le rang.

rare, rare ; **rarely**, rarement.

rascal (*playful*), le polisson ; (*serious*) le coquin, le scélérat.

rat, le rat.

rather, assez, plutôt.

ray, le rayon.

to reach, arriver à, parvenir à ; atteindre (craindre).

reach (*noun*), la portée ; **out of reach**, hors de portée.

to read, lire (*irr.*) ; **to read through** (*rapidly*), parcourir, *e.g.* il parcourut la lettre ; **to re-read**, relire ; **reader** (*person*), le lecteur, *f.* la lectrice ; **reading**, la lecture.

ready, prêt ; **ready to (do)**, prêt à (faire) ; **to get ready to (do)**, se préparer (se disposer *or* s'apprêter) à (faire).

real, réel, *f.* réelle ; (=*undoubted*) véritable, *e.g.* **a real rogue**, un véritable coquin ; **really**, réellement, vraiment ; **reality**, la réalité ; **in reality**, en réalité.

to realize, comprendre, se rendre compte de, *e.g.* alors il comprit (il se rendit compte de) son erreur.

to re-appear, reparaître (connaître).

reason, la raison ; le motif ; **reasonable**, raisonnable.

to re-assure, rassurer.

to recall, rappeler.

to recede, reculer, s'enfuir (fuir).

to receive, recevoir (*irr.*) ; (*socially*) accueillir (cueillir) ; **reception**, la réception, un accueil.

recent, récent ; **recently**, récemment.

to reckon, compter, calculer.

to recognize, reconnaître (connaître).

to recoil, reculer.

recollection, le souvenir.

to recommence, recommencer.

record (*gramophone*), le disque.

to recover (*from shock, etc.*), se remettre ; (*from illness*) se rétablir (finir).

recreation, la récréation.

red, rouge ; (*hair*) roux, *f.* rousse ; **to redden**, rougir (finir).

to reduce, réduire (conduire) ; **reduction**, la réduction.

to re-enter, rentrer (*with* être).

refrigerator, le réfrigérateur.

refuge, le refuge ; **to take refuge**, se réfugier.

to refuse, refuser, *e.g.* je refuse de le croire ; **refusal**, le refus.

regiment, le régiment.

region, la région.

to register, enregistrer.

to regret, regretter.

regular, régulier ; **regularly**, régulièrement.

regulation, le règlement.

reign, le règne ; **in the reign of**, sous le règne de ; **to reign**, régner.

rejoicings, les réjouissances (*f.*).

to rejoin, rejoindre (craindre).
to relate, raconter, conter.
relation, relative, le parent, *f.* la parente.
to relieve, soulager.
to remain, rester (*with* être).
to remark, remarquer ; faire remarquer ; **remarkable**, remarquable.
to remember, se souvenir de, *e.g.* je me souviens de son nom ; se rappeler, *e.g.* je me rappelle son nom.
remote (=*distant*), lointain ; (=*isolated*) isolé.
to remove (=*take away*), enlever ; (*to another house*) déménager.
to rend, déchirer.
to render, rendre (vendre).
to renew, renouveler.
to rent, louer ; **rent** (*to pay*), le loyer.
to repair, réparer ; **repair** (*noun*), la réparation.
to repeat, répéter.
to repel, repousser.
to repent, se repentir (de) (*conj. like* dormir).
to replace, remplacer.
reply, la réponse ; **to reply**, répondre (vendre), *e.g.* je réponds à votre question ; répliquer.
report, le rapport ; **to report**, rapporter.
to represent, représenter.
reproach, le reproche ; **to reproach**, reprocher, *e.g.* je lui reproche son indifférence.
to repulse, repousser.
request, la demande, la prière ; **to request**, prier, demander.
to require, vouloir, désirer.
rescue (*from water or fire*), le sauvetage.
to resemble, ressembler à, *e.g.* tu ressembles à ton père.
resignation, la résignation ; **resigned**, résigné.
to resist, résister (à), *e.g.* nous résistons aux attaques.
to resolve, résoudre (*irr.*) ; **he was resolved to win**, il était résolu à gagner.
to respect, respecter ; **in all respects**, sous tous les rapports ; **respectable**, convenable.
to resound, retentir (finir).
responsible, responsable ; **responsibility**, la responsabilité.
to rest, se reposer ; **rest**, le repos.
rest (=*remaining portion*), le reste ; (=*the others*) les autres, *e.g.* où sont les autres ?
restaurant, le restaurant ; **restaurant-car**, le wagon-restaurant.
result, le résultat.
to resume, reprendre, continuer.
to retire (=*withdraw*), se retirer ; (*from work*) prendre sa retraite ; **retirement**, la retraite.
to retort, répliquer.
to retrace one's steps, rebrousser chemin, revenir sur ses pas.
retreat, la retraite ; **to retreat, to beat a retreat**, battre en retraite.
return, le retour, (*to school*) la rentrée ; **on my return**, à mon retour.
to return (=*go back*), retourner (*with* être) ; (=*come back*) revenir (*with* être).
revenge, la vengeance ; **to take one's revenge, to revenge oneself**, se venger.
revolution, la révolution.
revolver, le revolver.
reward, la récompense ; **to**

reward (for), récompenser (de), *e.g.* il les récompensa de leurs services.

rib, la côte.

ribbon, le ruban.

rich, riche.

rid ; **to get rid of**, se débarrasser de.

ridiculous, ridicule.

to ride a horse, monter à cheval ; **(horse-) rider**, le cavalier ; **to ride a bicycle**, monter (rouler) à bicyclette ; **I cycled there**, j'y suis allé à bicyclette ; **to go for a cycle (motor, horse) ride**, se promener à bicyclette (en automobile, à cheval).

rifle, le fusil ; **rifle-shot**, le coup de fusil.

right (*=on the right hand*), droit ; (*=correct*) exact ; **on** (*or* **to**) **the right**, à droite ; **the right road**, le bon chemin ; **to be right**, avoir raison ; **all right!** très bien! fort bien!

to ring, sonner ; **I have rung for the maid**, j'ai sonné la bonne ; **to ring out** (*shots, etc.*), retentir (finir).

ring (*for finger*), la bague ; (*others*) un anneau.

riot, une émeute.

ripe, mûr ; **to ripen**, mûrir (finir).

ripple (*water*), la ride ; **to ripple**, se rider.

to rise, se lever ; (*buildings, etc.*) se dresser ; (*hills, mountains*) s'élever.

risk, le risque ; **to run risks**, courir des risques ; **to risk**, risquer ; **to risk one's life**, risquer la vie.

river (*great*), le fleuve ; (*smaller*) la rivière.

Riviera ; **the French Riviera**, la Côte d'Azur.

road (*in town*), la rue ; (*in country*) la route, le chemin ; **by the roadside**, au bord de la route (du chemin) ; **roadway**, la chaussée.

to roam, errer, rôder.

to roar (*water, etc.*), mugir (finir) ; (*beasts*) rugir (finir) ; **roar(ing)**, (*water, wind, etc.*) le mugissement, (*beasts*) le rugissement.

to roast, rôtir (finir) ; **roast** (*meat*), le rôti.

to rob, voler ; **robber**, le voleur.

robin, le rouge-gorge.

robust, robuste.

rock, le rocher.

rogue, le coquin.

to roll, rouler ; (*intrans.*) se rouler, *e.g.* il se roulait sur l'herbe.

roof, le toit.

rook, la corneille ; **rookery**, la colonie de corneilles.

room, (*any room*) la pièce ; **dining-room**, la salle à manger ; **drawing-room**, le salon ; **bedroom**, la chambre (à coucher) ; **bathroom**, la salle de bains ; **room** (*=space*), la place, *e.g.* y a-t-il de la place?

root, la racine.

rope, la corde.

rose, la rose.

rough, (*road*) raboteux ; (*sea*) gros, *f.* grosse ; (*manners, blows, etc.*) rude.

round (*adj.*), rond ; (*prep.*) autour de ; **to look (turn) round**, se retourner ; **to go round**, faire le tour de ; **round** (*postman's, etc.*), la tournée.

roundabout (*traffic*), le rond-point.

to row, ramer ; **to go for a row**,

faire une partie de canot (canotage) ; **rowing-boat,** le canot, une embarcation.

to rub, frotter.

rubber, le caoutchouc ; (*erasing*) la gomme.

rude, impoli ; (=*coarse*) grossier.

to ruin (=*damage*), abîmer.

rule, le règlement.

ruler, la règle.

to rumble, gronder ; **rumble, rumbling,** le grondement.

to run, courir (*irr.*) ; **to run away,** se sauver, s'enfuir (fuir) ; **to run for, to run and get,** courir chercher ; **to run up** (=*approach*), accourir ; **to run up** (*e.g. stairs*), monter en courant ; **to run down,** descendre en courant ; **to run in,** entrer en courant ; **to run out,** sortir en courant ; **to run across,** traverser en courant ; **to run over** (=*crush*), écraser.

to rush, se précipiter, se ruer.

Russia, la Russie ; **Russian,** le (la) Russe ; (*adj.*) russe.

rustling, le bruissement.

S

sacrifice, le sacrifice.

sad, triste ; **sadness,** la tristesse.

saddle, la selle.

safe, sûr, sauf ; **safe and sound,** sain et sauf ; **safety,** la sûreté, la sécurité ; **in safety,** en sûreté, en sécurité.

sail, la voile ; **to sail** (=*travel*), naviguer ; (=*to go in for sailing*) faire de la voile.

sailor (*any rank*), le marin ; (= *seaman*) le matelot.

saint, le saint ; **All Saints' Day** (Nov. 1), la Toussaint.

salad, la salade.

salary, le traitement.

sale, la vente ; **on sale,** en vente.

salt, le sel.

same, même ; **all the same,** tout de même, quand même ; **to do the same,** en faire autant, *e.g.* ils en ont fait autant ; **it is all the same to me,** cela m'est égal.

sand, le sable.

to satisfy, satisfaire (faire) ; **satisfied,** satisfait, content ; **to be satisfied with (doing),** se contenter de (faire).

Saturday, samedi (*m.*) ; **last Saturday,** samedi dernier ; **next Saturday,** samedi prochain.

saucepan, la casserole.

saucer, la soucoupe.

sausage (*small*), la saucisse ; **dinner-sausage,** le saucisson.

savage, féroce.

to save, sauver ; (*money*) épargner, économiser ; **savings,** les économies (*f.*).

save (=*except*), sauf.

to say, dire (*irr.*) ; **that is to say,** c'est-à-dire ; **I say!** dites (dis) donc!

to scale (*e.g. a wall*), escalader.

scamp, le polisson.

scar, la cicatrice.

scarce, rare.

scarcely, à peine.

to scare, effrayer, épouvanter ; faire peur, *e.g.* vous m'avez fait peur.

scarf, le cache-nez.

to scatter, éparpiller.

scent, le parfum ; **these flowers give out a delightful scent,** ces fleurs répandent un parfum délicieux ; **to scent** (=*perfume*), parfumer ; (=*detect by smell*) flairer.

scheme, le projet.
scholarship, la bourse.
school, une école ; **schoolboy**, un écolier ; **schoolgirl**, une écolière ; **high school, grammar school**, le lycée, (*smaller*) le collège ; **school-friend**, un(e) ami(e) de classe, un(e) camarade de classe.
scissors, les ciseaux (*m.*).
to **scold**, gronder.
to **scorn**, mépriser, dédaigner.
Scotland, l'Écosse (*f.*) ; **Scotsman**, un Écossais ; **Scotswoman**, une Écossaise ; **Scottish**, écossais.
to **scratch**, gratter.
scream, le cri (perçant) ; **to scream**, crier, pousser des cris.
screen (*cinema*), l'écran (*m.*).
sea, la mer ; **sea-side**, le bord de la mer.
seaman, le matelot.
to **search (for)**, chercher ; **to search** (=*inspect*), fouiller ; **in search of**, à la recherche de.
season, la saison.
seat (=*form, bench*), le banc ; (*in train or car*) la banquette ; (=*place for one person*) la place ; **to take a seat**, prendre place.
second (*of time*), la seconde.
second (*adj.*), second, deuxième ; **second-hand**, d'occasion, *e.g.* un livre d'occasion.
secret, le secret ; (*adj.*) secret, *f.* secrète.
to **see**, voir (*irr.*) ; **to see again**, revoir ; **see to it that . . .**, veillez à ce que +*subj.* ; **seeing that**, vu que, puisque.
to **seek**, chercher.
to **seem**, sembler, paraître (connaître) ; **it seems to me that**, il me semble que ; **I seem to have read it before**, il me semble que je l'ai déjà lu *or* il me semble l'avoir déjà lu.
to **seize**, saisir (finir).
seldom, rarement.
to **select**, choisir (finir).
to **sell**, vendre.
to **send**, envoyer (*fut.* j'enverrai) ; **to send for**, envoyer chercher ; **to send back**, renvoyer ; **to send away**, renvoyer, congédier.
sense, le sens ; **sensible**, sensé ; **sensitive**, sensible.
sentence, la phrase.
sentinelle, la sentinelle.
to **separate**, séparer ; (*intrans.*) se séparer, *e.g.* ils se séparèrent à minuit ; **separate** (*adj.*), séparé.
September, septembre ; **in September**, en septembre, au mois de septembre.
sergeant, le sergent.
serious, sérieux, grave.
servant, le (la) domestique ; le serviteur.
to **serve**, servir (dormir) ; **to serve to (do)**, servir à (faire) ; **to serve as**, servir de, *e.g.* cette pièce servait de cuisine.
service, le service ; **I do him a service**, je lui rends service.
serviette, la serviette.
to **set** (=*place*), mettre, poser ; **to set down**, déposer ; **to set off** (=*depart*), partir (*with* être).
to **settle** (*questions, bills, etc.*), régler ; (*in a place or house*) s'installer.
several, plusieurs, *e.g.* plusieurs hommes, plusieurs femmes.
severe, sévère ; **severely**, sévèrement.
to **sew**, coudre (*irr.*).

shade, l'ombre (*f.*); **in the shade,** à l'ombre.

shadow, l'ombre (*f.*).

to shake, secouer; **I shake hands with the doctor,** je serre la main au docteur.

shallow, peu profond.

shame, la honte; **shameful,** honteux.

shape, la forme.

share, la part; **to share,** partager.

sharp (=*acute*), aigu, *f.* aiguë; (=*quick*) vif. *f.* vive; **sharply** (=*quickly*), vivement; (=*in an abrupt tone*) sèchement.

to shave, se raser.

shed, le hangar; (*for farm animals*) une étable.

to shed (*light*), verser.

sheep, le mouton.

sheer, à pic, *e.g.* une falaise à pic; **to fall sheer,** descendre à pic.

sheet, le drap; (*of paper*) la feuille.

shelf, le rayon.

shell, la coquille; **shellfish,** le coquillage.

shelter, un abri; **to shelter,** abriter.

shepherd, le berger; **shepherdess,** la bergère.

to shift, bouger; (*a thing*) déplacer.

to shine, briller.

ship, le navire; **ship-wreck,** le naufrage; **to be (ship-) wrecked,** faire naufrage.

shirt, la chemise.

to shiver, frissonner; (*with cold*) grelotter.

to shock, scandaliser.

shoe, le soulier; **brown shoes,** les souliers jaunes; **shoe-repairer,** le cordonnier.

to shoot (*game*), chasser; **shooting** (*game*), la chasse.

shop (*large*), le magasin; (*small*) la boutique; **shop-window,** la vitrine; **shopkeeper,** le marchand, *f.* la marchande; **to do some shopping,** faire des emplettes.

shore, le rivage.

short, court; (*of persons*) petit; **to stop short,** s'arrêter court; **short story,** le conte; **in short (brief),** bref, enfin; **shorts** (*dress*), le short.

shot, le coup de fusil (pistolet); **to fire a shot,** tirer un coup (de fusil, de pistolet).

shoulder, une épaule; **to shrug one's shoulders,** hausser les épaules.

shout, le cri; **to shout,** crier; **to give a shout,** pousser un cri.

shovel, la pelle.

show (*theatre*), le spectacle.

to show, montrer, indiquer, faire voir; **to show up,** faire monter, *e.g.* faites monter ce monsieur; **to show in,** faire entrer, *e.g.* faites entrer ce monsieur.

shower, une averse; **shower(-bath),** la douche; **to have a shower,** prendre une douche.

shriek, le cri; **to shriek,** pousser des cris (perçants).

Shrove Tuesday, le mardi gras.

to shrug one's shoulders, hausser les épaules.

to shut, fermer; **the door shuts,** la porte se ferme; **to shut in,** enfermer.

shutter, le volet, le contrevent.

shy, timide.

sick, malade; **sick person,** le (la) malade.

side, le côté ; **on this side**, de ce côté ; **on the other side**, de l'autre côté ; **at my side**, à mes côtés ; **side by side**, côte à côte ; **by the side of** (*e.g. a river*), au bord de.

sideboard, le buffet.

sidewalk (*pavement*), le trottoir.

sigh, le soupir ; **to sigh**, soupirer.

sight, la vue, le spectacle ; **I know him by sight**, je le connais de vue ; **I have lost sight of him**, je l'ai perdu de vue ; **to catch sight of**, apercevoir (recevoir).

sign, le signe ; **to make a sign to**, faire signe à, *e.g.* je leur ai fait signe ; **to sign**, signer.

to signify, signifier.

silent, silencieux ; **to be (become) silent**, se taire (*irr.*) ; **silence**, le silence.

silk, la soie.

silly, stupide, bête, sot, *f.* sotte ; **silly act**, la sottise.

similar, semblable ; pareil, *f.* pareille.

simple, simple ; (=*ingenuous*) naïf, *f.* naïve ; **simplicity**, la simplicité.

since, depuis ; **since** (*conj.*), depuis que, *e.g.* depuis que je suis ici ; (=*seeing that*) puisque, *e.g.* puisque vous partez.

to sing, chanter ; **singer**, le chanteur, *f.* la chanteuse.

single, seul ; **not a single**, ne . . . aucun(e), *e.g.* on ne voit aucune maison.

to sip, déguster.

sir, monsieur.

sister, la sœur ; **sister-in-law**, la belle-sœur.

to sit (down), s'asseoir (*irr.*) ; **sitting**, assis ; **I sit down** (*act*), je m'assieds ; **I am sitting** (*state*), je suis assis ; **to sit up**, se redresser ; **to sit down at table**, se mettre à table.

situation, la situation ; **to be situated**, être situé, se trouver ; **this village is situated 15 kilometres from Orleans**, ce village est situé (se trouve) à 15 kilomètres d'Orléans.

size, la dimension ; **great size**, la grandeur, la grosseur.

skates, les patins (*m.*) ; **to skate**, patiner.

skilful, adroit.

skin, la peau.

skirt, la jupe.

sky, le ciel, *pl.* les cieux.

slab (*of stone*), la dalle.

to slam a door, faire claquer une porte.

slave, un(e) esclave.

to sleep, dormir (*irr.*) ; (=*spend the night*) coucher, *e.g.* j'ai couché à l'hôtel ; **sleep**, le sommeil ; **to go to sleep**, s'endormir (dormir) ; **to be (feel) sleepy**, avoir sommeil.

sleeve, la manche.

slice, la tranche ; **slice of bread** (*with butter or jam*), la tartine.

to slide, glisser.

slight, léger ; **slightest** (=*least*), le (la) moindre, *e.g.* sans la moindre difficulté.

slim, mince, svelte.

to slip, glisser ; **to slip away**, se dérober, s'esquiver ; **slippery**, glissant.

slipper, la pantoufle.

slope, la pente.

slow, lent ; **slowly**, lentement ; **slowness**, la lenteur ; **to slow down**, ralentir (finir).

to slumber, sommeiller.
sly, rusé, malin, *f.* maligne.
small, petit.
smart (*appearance*), élégant.
to smash, briser, casser.
smell, une odeur ; (=*perfume*) le parfum ; **to smell**, sentir (dormir) ; **that smells nice**, cela sent bon ; **that smells bad (nasty)**, cela sent mauvais.
to smile, sourire (rire) ; **smile** (*noun*), le sourire.
smock, la blouse.
smoke, la fumée ; **to smoke**, fumer.
smooth, uni.
smuggler, le contrebandier.
snare, le piège.
to snatch, arracher, *e.g.* il arracha le bâton à l'homme.
to snore, ronfler.
snow, la neige ; **snowflake**, le flocon de neige ; **to snow**, neiger ; **it snows**, il neige ; **it was snowing**, il neigeait ; **it had snowed**, il avait neigé.
so, si, *e.g.* c'est si joli ; **so** (=*therefore*), donc ; **so** (=*to such an extent*), tellement, *e.g.* je suis tellement fatigué ; **so much (many)**, tant ; **so that** (=*in order that*), pour que *or* afin que +*subj.* *e.g.* pour qu'il puisse sortir.
to soak, tremper ; **soaked to the skin**, trempé jusqu'aux os.
soap, le savon.
sob, le sanglot ; **to sob**, sangloter.
society, la société.
sock, la chaussette.
sofa, le divan.
soft, doux, *f.* douce ; (=*soft to the touch*) mou, *f.* molle ; (=*easy-going*) indulgent ; **softly**, doucement ; **softness**, la douceur ; **soft-hearted**, tendre ; **to soften**, adoucir (finir) ; (*feelings*) attendrir (finir).
soil, le sol.
soldier, le soldat.
sole (*of shoe*), la semelle.
sole (*adj.*), seul ; (=*one and only*) unique, *e.g.* le survivant unique.
solid, solide.
some (*pronoun*), en, *e.g.* En avez-vous? —Oui, j'en ai.
some (*partitive article*), du, de la, de l' *or* des, *e.g.* du pain, de la viande, de l'eau, des fruits ; **some more bread**, encore du pain.
some (*unspecified*), quelque, *e.g.* je l'ai lu dans quelque journal ; **some distance away**, à quelque distance ; **some** (=*a few*), quelques, *e.g.* c'est à quelques kilomètres ; **someone, somebody**, quelqu'un ; **someone else**, quelqu'un d'autre ; **something**, quelque chose ; **something good**, quelque chose de bon ; **sometimes**, quelquefois ; **somewhere**, quelque part ; **somewhere else**, ailleurs ; **somewhat**, un peu, quelque peu ; **somebody or other**, je ne sais qui ; **something or other** je ne sais quoi ; **somehow (or other)**, je ne sais comment ; **some reason or other**, je ne sais quelle raison.
son, le fils ; **son-in-law**, le gendre.
song (*with words*), la chanson ; (*birds'*) le chant.
soon, bientôt ; **so soon**, si tôt ; **too soon**, trop tôt ; **sooner**, plus tôt ; **sooner or later**, tôt

ou tard ; **he soon came back,** il ne tarda pas à revenir ; **I will see you soon!** à bientôt! **as soon as,** dès que, aussitôt que.

sorrow, le chagrin.

sorry ; to be sorry, regretter, *e.g.* je regrette de refuser; **sorry!** pardon!

sort, la sorte, une espèce.

sou, le sou.

soul, une âme.

sound, le bruit ; (*bells, music, etc.*) le son.

soup, la soupe; (*clear*) le potage; **soup-tureen,** la soupière.

south, le sud ; **the South of France,** le Midi de la France.

space, l'espace (*m.*) ; **spacious,** spacieux.

spade, la bêche.

Spain, l'Espagne (*f.*) ; **Spanish,** espagnol ; **Spaniard,** un Espagnol, une Espagnole.

spark, une étincelle.

to sparkle, étinceler.

sparrow, le moineau.

to speak, parler.

species, une espèce.

spectacles, les lunettes (*f.*).

spectator, le spectateur.

speech, le discours ; (*=faculty of speech*) la parole.

speed, la vitesse ; **at full speed,** à toute vitesse.

to spend (*money*), dépenser ; (*time*) passer.

to spill (*liquids*), répandre (vendre); (*=overturn*) renverser.

spinster, la vieille fille.

spire, la flèche.

spirit, l'esprit (*m.*).

to spit, cracher.

in spite of, malgré.

to split, fendre (vendre).

to spoil, gâter ; **spoilt,** gâté.

spoon, la cuiller *or* la cuillère.

sport, le sport ; **sports ground,** le terrain de sport, le stade ; **sportsman** (*=hunter*), le chasseur.

spot (*=place*), un endroit, le coin ; (*=mark*) la tache ; **on the spot,** sur place.

to spread (*plains, sea, etc.*), s'étendre (vendre) ; (*=give out, scatter*) répandre (vendre).

spring (*water*), la source.

spring (*season*), le printemps ; **in spring,** au printemps ; **a spring morning,** un matin de printemps.

spy, un espion.

square, carré.

square (*in a town*), la place.

to squeeze, serrer.

to squint, loucher.

stable, une écurie.

stadium, le stade.

staff (*=employees*), le personnel.

stage (*theatre*), la scène.

stage-coach, la diligence.

to stagger, chanceler.

to stain, tacher.

stained-glass window, le vitrail, *pl.* les vitraux.

stairs, staircase, un escalier ; **stair** (*single*), la marche.

stalk, la tige.

to stammer, balbutier.

stamp (*postage*), le timbre.

to stamp (one's foot), frapper du pied ; **to stamp about** (*e.g. in snow*), piétiner.

to stand (*of persons*), se tenir ; se placer ; (*buildings, etc.*) se dresser ; **to stand up,** se lever, se mettre debout ; **to stand upright,** se tenir debout ; **to stand** (*in an attitude or state*), rester, demeurer.

standing (*of persons*), debout ; **he was standing,** il était debout ; **standing** (*of things*), posé, placé.

star, une étoile, un astre ; **to sleep under the stars,** coucher à la belle étoile.

to stare at, regarder fixement.

to start (=*depart*), partir (*with* être) ; **to start to** (do), commencer à (faire), se mettre à (faire) ; **to start off,** se mettre en route (en marche) ; **to start along a street,** s'engager dans une rue ; **to start over a bridge,** s'engager sur un pont ; **to start** (=*be startled*), sursauter, tressaillir (*irr.*) ; **start** (=*beginning*) le commencement, le début.

startled, effaré.

starving, affamé.

state, un état ; **statesman,** un homme d'État.

station (*railway*), la gare ; **station-master,** le chef de gare.

stature, la taille.

to stay, rester (*with* être) ; demeurer.

stay (=*sojourn, period*), le séjour.

steak, le bifteck.

to steal, voler, dérober ; **they stole his money from him,** ils lui volèrent son argent.

steamer (*passenger*), le paquebot.

steel, l'acier (*m.*).

steep, raide, escarpé.

to steer, diriger ; **steering-wheel** (*of car*), le volant.

steer (=*bullock*), le bœuf.

stem, la tige.

steps, un escalier ; **step** (=*single step*), la marche ; **door-step,** le pas de la porte ; **step** (=*pace*), le pas ; **to quicken one's step,** presser le pas ; **to retrace one's steps,** revenir sur ses pas ; rebrousser chemin.

sternly, sévèrement.

stewpot, la marmite.

stick, le bâton ; **walking-stick,** la canne.

stiff, raide.

to stifle, étouffer ; **stifling,** étouffant.

still, encore, toujours.

to sting, piquer.

to stir (*liquids, etc.*), remuer.

stocking, le bas.

stone, la pierre ; (=*pebble*) le caillou (*pl.* -x) ; **stonemason,** le maçon.

to stoop (down), se baisser.

stop, un arrêt.

to stop, (s') arrêter, *e.g.* il arrête sa voiture ; la voiture s'arrête ; (=*cease*) cesser ; **to stop** (doing), s'arrêter (cesser) de (faire), *e.g.* il s'arrêta (cessa) de crier ; **to stop** (=*prevent*), empêcher, *e.g.* je les empêcherai de sortir.

store (=*large shop*), le magasin.

storey (=*floor*), un étage.

storm (=*tempest*), la tempête ; (*thunderstorm*) un orage.

story, une histoire ; **short story,** le conte; **detective story,** le roman policier.

stout, gros, *f.* grosse.

stove (*paraffin*), le réchaud.

straight, droit ; **go straight on,** allez tout droit ; **to put straight** (=*tidy*), ranger.

straightway, immédiatement, aussitôt.

strange, étrange, singulier ; **stranger,** un inconnu.

straw, la paille.
strawberry, la fraise.
to stray, s'égarer.
stream, la rivière.
street, la rue ; **street-lamp**, le réverbère.
strength, la force *or* les forces ; **with all my strength**, de toutes mes forces.
to stretch (out), s'étendre (vendre) ; **stretched out**, étendu.
strewn with, jonché de.
to strike, frapper ; (*clocks*) sonner ; **to strike hard**, frapper dur ; **to strike down**, abattre (battre).
string, la ficelle.
to strive to (do), chercher à (faire), s'efforcer de (faire).
stroke, le coup ; **on the stroke of nine**, sur le coup de neuf heures, à neuf heures précises.
to stroke, caresser, flatter.
stroll, le tour ; **to go for a stroll**, faire un tour, faire une petite promenade ; **to stroll** (*idly*), flâner ; **stroller**, le promeneur.
strong, fort ; solide.
struggle, la lutte ; **to struggle** (=*strive*), lutter ; (=*make wild efforts*) se débattre.
stubborn, entêté.
study, (*work*) l'étude (*f.*) ; (*room*) le cabinet de travail ; **to study**, étudier ; **student**, un(e) étudiant(e).
stuff (*cloth*), une étoffe.
to stumble, trébucher.
stupid, stupide.
suburbs, la banlieue.
to succeed (=*have success*), réussir (finir) ; **to succeed in (doing)**, réussir à (faire), arriver à (faire), parvenir à (faire) ; **to succeed** (=*come after*), succéder à, *e.g.* une journée calme succéda à cette nuit de tempête.
success, le succès ; **to be successful**, réussir (finir), avoir du succès.
such, tel, *f.* telle, *e.g.* une telle chose, *pl.* de telles choses ; pareil, *f.* pareille, *e.g.* des choses pareilles ; **such a pretty child**, un si joli enfant ; **such as**, tel que.
sudden, soudain, subit ; (*movements, etc.*) brusque ; **suddenly**, tout à coup, soudain, soudainement, subitement ; brusquement.
suede, le suède.
to suffer, souffrir (ouvrir) ; **suffering**, la souffrance.
to suffice, suffire (*irr.*) ; **sufficient**, suffisant ; **sufficiently**, suffisamment.
sugar, le sucre.
to suggest, suggérer, proposer.
suit, le complet ; (*woman's*) le tailleur ; **suit-case**, la valise.
to suit, convenir (venir), *e.g.* cette date ne nous convient pas ; aller, *e.g.* ce chapeau ne lui va pas ; **suitable**, convenable.
sum (=*amount*), la somme ; (=*calculation*) le calcul.
summer, l'été (*m.*) ; **in summer**, en été ; **a summer('s) day**, un jour d'été.
summit, le sommet.
sun, le soleil ; **sunshine**, le soleil ; **in the sun**, au soleil ; **the sun rises**, le soleil se lève ; **the sun sets**, le soleil se couche ; **sunrise**, le lever du soleil ; **sunset**, le coucher du soleil ; **sundial**, le cadran solaire ; **sunshade**, une ombrelle ; **sun-**

burnt (tanned), bruni, bronzé.

Sunday, dimanche (*m.*) ; **last Sunday,** dimanche dernier.

superfluous, superflu.

superintendent (of police), le commissaire (de police).

superior, supérieur.

supermarket, le supermarché.

to supervise, surveiller ; **supervision,** la surveillance.

supper, le souper.

to supply, fournir (finir).

to support (=*hold up*), soutenir (tenir), supporter ; (=*maintain*) entretenir (tenir).

to suppose, supposer.

sure, sûr ; **surely,** sûrement ; **to make sure that,** s'assurer que.

surprise, la surprise, l'étonnement (*m.*) ; **I give them a surprise,** je leur fais une surprise ; **to surprise,** surprendre (prendre), étonner ; **to be surprised,** s'étonner ; **surprising,** surprenant, étonnant.

to surrender, se rendre (vendre).

to surround, entourer ; **surrounded by,** entouré de.

surroundings, les environs (*m.*), les alentours (*m.*).

to survive, survivre (à), *e.g.* elle survécut à son mari.

to suspect, soupconner, se douter de.

suspender-belt, le porte-jarretelles.

suspicion, le soupçon; **suspicious** (=*feeling suspicion*), soupçonneux, méfiant; (=*arousing suspicion*) suspect.

swallow, une hirondelle.

to swallow, avaler.

to sway (*movement*), se balancer.

sweat, la sueur ; **to sweat,** suer ; **sweating,** en sueur.

to sweep (*with broom*), balayer.

sweet, le bonbon.

sweet (*adj.*), doux, *f.* douce ; **sweetly,** doucement ; **sweet** (*tasting*), sucré.

swift, rapide ; **swiftly,** rapidement.

to swim, nager ; **to swim across a river,** traverser (passer) une rivière à la nage; **swim-suit,** le maillot de bain; **swimming pool,** la piscine; **swimming-trunks,** le caleçon de bain.

to switch on the light, allumer l'électricité ; **to switch off,** couper l'électricité ; **to switch off the engine** (*of a car*), couper l'allumage.

Switzerland, la Suisse ; **Swiss** (*man*), le Suisse ; (*woman*) la Suissesse ; **Swiss** (*adj.*), suisse.

sword, une épée.

T

table, la table ; **at table,** à table ; **table-cloth,** la nappe ; **table-cover,** le tapis ; **to lay the table,** mettre la table (le couvert) ; **to sit down at table,** se mettre à table.

tail, la queue.

tailor, le tailleur.

to take, prendre (*irr.*) ; (=*carry*) porter, *e.g.* portez ces lettres à M. Muche ; **to take** (*a person*), mener, emmener, *e.g.* sa mère le mena chez le dentiste ; je les ai emmenés à Versailles ; **to take back,** reprendre ; **to take away,** emporter ; **to take off,** ôter ; **to take up,** monter (*with* avoir) ; **to take down,** descendre (*with* avoir) ; **to**

take out, sortir (*with* avoir), tirer, *e.g.* il sortit (tira) une clef de sa poche, *or* il prit une clef dans sa poche ; **he took his book from him,** il lui prit son livre; **to take after** (=*resemble*), tenir de.

talcum powder, le talc.

to **talk,** parler ; **talkative,** bavard ; **talk** (*noun*), une conversation, un entretien.

tall (*person*), grand; (*thing*) haut.

tank (*mil.*), le char (d'assaut).

tap, le robinet.

task, la tâche.

taste, le goût ; **to taste,** goûter.

taxi, le taxi.

tea, le thé ; **to have tea,** prendre le thé ; **tea-pot,** la théière.

to **teach,** apprendre (prendre), *e.g.* je lui apprends à nager ; (*in school*) enseigner, *e.g.* je leur enseigne le latin ; **teaching,** l'enseignement (*m.*) ; **teacher** (*secondary or university*), le professeur ; (*primary*) un instituteur, *f.* une institutrice.

team, une équipe ; (*of horses*) un attelage.

tear (*weeping*), la larme ; **to burst into tears,** fondre en larmes (en pleurs).

to **tear,** déchirer ; **to tear out,** arracher.

to **tease,** taquiner.

telegram, le télégramme, la dépêche.

telephone, le téléphone ; **to telephone,** téléphoner.

television, la télévision ; **television set,** le poste de télévision, le téléviseur.

to **tell,** dire (*irr.*), *e.g.* je lui dis d'attendre ; (=*relate*) raconter, conter.

temper (=*anger*), la colère ; **to lose one's temper,** se mettre en colère, s'emporter; **good- (bad-) tempered,** de bonne (mauvaise) humeur.

tempest, la tempête.

to **tempt,** tenter ; **temptation,** la tentation.

tenant, le locataire.

tender (*adj.*), tendre ; **tenderly,** tendrement.

to **tender** (*money, etc.*), tendre (vendre).

tennis, le tennis ; **to play tennis,** jouer au tennis.

tent, la tente.

tepid, tiède.

term (*school*), le trimestre.

terrace, la terrasse.

terrific, formidable.

to **terrify,** épouvanter ; **terrifying,** épouvantable.

terror, la terreur.

test, une épreuve ; (*school*) la composition ; **to test,** éprouver, mettre à l'épreuve.

than, que ; **more than 1000 francs,** plus de 1000 francs ; **I eat more than you,** je mange plus que vous.

to **thank (for),** remercier (de), *e.g.* je vous remercie de votre lettre ; **thank you,** merci ; **thank you very much,** merci beaucoup ; **thanks,** les remerciements (*m.*) ; **thanks to,** grâce à ; **to give thanks to God,** rendre grâces à Dieu.

theatre, le théâtre.

theft, le vol.

then (=*at that time*), alors ; (=*next*) puis ; (=*afterwards*) ensuite ; (=*therefore*) donc ; **until then,** jusque-là, jusqu' alors.

there, y, *e.g.* il y est ; là, *e.g.* il est là ; **there she is!** la voilà! **over there**, là-bas ; **up there**, là-haut ; **in there**, là-dedans.

therefore, donc.

thereupon, là-dessus.

thick, épais, *f.* épaisse.

thief, le voleur.

thin (*person*), maigre.

thing, la chose ; **something**, quelque chose.

to **think**, penser, croire ; (=*reflect*) réfléchir (finir) ; (=*ponder*) songer ; **I am thinking about my work**, je pense (je réfléchis, je songe) à mon travail ; **what do you think of my car?** que pensez-vous de ma voiture?

third (*part*), le tiers.

thirst, la soif ; **to be thirsty**, avoir soif ; **to be very thirsty**, avoir très soif, avoir grand'soif.

thoroughly, à fond, *e.g.* il connaît ce système à fond.

as **though** (**if**), comme si ; **as though to**, comme pour, *e.g.* il s'arrêta comme pour me parler.

thought, la pensée ; **thoughtless**, étourdi.

thousand, mille ; **5000**, cinq mille ; **thousands of (cars)**, des milliers de (voitures) ; **a few thousand francs**, quelques milliers de francs.

threat, la menace ; **to threaten to (do)**, menacer de (faire).

threshold, le seuil.

thrilled, ému ; **thrilling**, émouvant, passionnant.

throat, la gorge.

through, par, à travers ; **to go (pass) through**, traverser.

to **throw**, jeter, lancer ; **to throw away**, jeter.

to **thrust in**, enfoncer, *e.g.* il enfonça son couteau dans le pain.

thumb, le pouce.

thunder, le tonnerre ; **thunder-storm**, un orage.

Thursday, jeudi (*m.*) ; **last Thursday**, jeudi dernier.

thus, ainsi.

ticket, le billet ; **I get my ticket**, je prends mon billet ; **ticket-inspector**, le contrôleur ; **ticket-office**, le guichet.

tide, la marée ; **at high tide**, à marée haute ; **at low tide**, à marée basse ; **the tide is in**, la mer est haute ; **the tide is out**, la mer est basse.

to **tidy (up)**, ranger.

tie, la cravate.

to **tie**, attacher ; (*in a knot*) nouer, *e.g.* je noue ma cravate.

tile (*roof*), la tuile ; (*floor, wall*) le carreau.

till, jusqu'à ; **till then**, jusque-là, jusqu'alors ; **I shall not leave till 2 o'clock**, je ne partirai pas avant 2 heures.

till (*for money*), la caisse.

time, le temps ; **a long time**, longtemps ; **all the time**, tout le temps, sans cesse ; **most of the time**, la plupart du temps ; **at the same time**, en même temps ; **from time to time**, de temps en temps ; **in time** (=*punctually*), à temps ; **in our time**, de nos jours ; **I have a good time**, je m'amuse bien ; **to spend (waste) one's time (doing)**, passer (perdre) son temps à (faire) ; **time-table** (*school*), un emploi du temps, (*railway, etc.*) un indicateur, un horaire.

time (=*period*), une époque.

time (*by the clock*), l'heure (*f.*) ; **what is the time?** quelle heure est-il? **at what time?** à quelle heure? **before time,** avant l'heure, en avance.
time (*as in* 3 *times, etc.*), la fois ; **three times a day,** trois fois par jour ; **at times,** parfois.
tin, la boîte.
tiny, tout petit.
tip, le pourboire.
tip-toe ; to walk on tip-toe, marcher sur la pointe des pieds.
to tire, fatiguer ; **to get tired,** se fatiguer ; **tired,** fatigué ; **tiring,** fatigant.
tiresome, ennuyeux.
tit for tat, à bon chat bon rat.
title, le titre.
tobacco, le tabac.
to-day, aujourd'hui.
together, ensemble ; **to bring together,** réunir (finir).
toil, le travail, la besogne ; **to toil,** travailler.
toilet (*W.C.*), le cabinet.
tomato, la tomate.
tomorrow, demain ; **tomorrow morning,** demain matin.
tone, le ton.
tonight, cette nuit ; (=*this evening*) ce soir.
too, trop ; **too much (many),** trop ; **too** (=*also*), aussi.
tool, un outil.
tooth, la dent ; **tooth-ache,** le mal aux dents ; **tooth-brush,** la brosse à dents.
top, le haut ; **at the top (of),** en haut (de) ; **top** (=*summit*), le sommet, la cime.
torch, la lampe de poche.
to torment, tourmenter.
torrent, le torrent ; **it rains in torrents,** il pleut à verse.
to touch, toucher ; **touching,** touchant.
tourist, le touriste.
towards, vers ; **to go towards,** se diriger vers ; **towards** (*of behaviour*), envers, *e.g.* respectueux envers ses maîtres.
towel, la serviette (de toilette) ; un essuie-mains.
tower, la tour ; **Eiffel Tower,** la tour Eiffel ; **church tower,** le clocher.
town, la ville ; **to go to (into) town,** aller en ville ; **Town Hall,** l'hôtel de ville.
toy, le jouet.
track (*railway*), la voie ; (=*trail*) la piste.
tractor, le tracteur.
trade, le commerce ; (=*occupation*) le métier.
traffic, la circulation, le mouvement ; **traffic-block,** un embouteillage ; **traffic lights,** les feux (de circulation).
train, le train ; **by train,** par le train ; **to catch a train,** prendre un train ; **the 6.30 train,** le train de 6h. 30 ; **fast train,** le rapide.
to translate, traduire (conduire) ; **translation,** la traduction.
to transport, transporter.
trap, le piège.
to travel, voyager ; (=*go along, of vehicles*) marcher, rouler ; **to travel across (through),** parcourir (courir) ; **traveller,** le voyageur.
tray, le plateau.
treasure, le trésor.
tree, un arbre.
to tremble, trembler.
trench, la tranchée.
trick, le tour ; **nasty trick,** un villain tour.

trigger, la détente.
trip, la promenade, une excursion ; **to go for a trip**, faire une promenade (une excursion).
troop, la troupe ; (=*gang of boys, etc.*) la bande.
trouble, la peine, le souci ; **to trouble**, déranger, (=*worry*) inquiéter, (=*impede*) gêner.
trousers (*short*), la culotte ; (*long*) le pantalon.
trout, la truite.
true, vrai ; **truly**, vraiment ; **truth**, la vérité ; **to speak the truth**, dire la vérité.
trunk (*tree*), le tronc ; (*luggage*) la malle ; **I pack my trunk**, je fais ma malle.
trust, la confiance ; **to trust to**, se fier à, *e.g.* je ne me fie pas à ses promesses.
to **try (to)**, essayer (de), tâcher (de), *e.g.* il essaya (tâcha) d'ouvrir la fenêtre ; **to try hard to** (do), s'efforcer de (faire) ; **to try on**, essayer, *e.g.* il essaie des souliers.
Tuesday, mardi (*m.*) ; **Shrove Tuesday**, le mardi gras.
tune, un air.
turf, le gazon.
turkey, le dindon, *f.* la dinde.
turn, le tour ; **in my turn**, à mon tour ; **in turn**, à tour de rôle ; **a good turn**, un service ; **I do him a good turn**, je lui rends service.
to **turn**, tourner ; **he turned to me**, il se tourna vers moi ; **to turn round**, se retourner ; **to turn about**, faire demi-tour ; **he turned me out**, il me mit à la porte.
twice, deux fois.
twinkling ; **in the twinkling of an eye**, en un clin d'œil.
tyre, le pneu.

U

ugly, laid, vilain.
umbrella, le parapluie.
unbearable, insupportable.
uncle, l'oncle.
to **uncover**, découvrir (couvrir).
under, sous.
to **undergo**, subir (finir).
to **understand**, comprendre (prendre).
to **undertake**, se charger de, entreprendre ; **to undertake to** (do), se charger de (faire), entreprendre de (faire).
to **undress (oneself)**, se déshabiller.
unexpected, inattendu.
unfortunate, malheureux ; **unfortunately**, malheureusement.
unfurnished, non meublé.
unhappy, malheureux ; **unhappily**, malheureusement ; **unhappiness**, le malheur.
uniform, l'uniforme (*m.*).
United States, les États-Unis (*m.*).
unknown, inconnu.
unless, à moins que (+ne *and subj.*), *e.g.* **unless you are in a hurry**, à moins que vous ne soyez pressé.
to **unload**, décharger.
unlucky ; **I am unlucky**, je n'ai pas de chance.
unmarried, non marié.
unpleasant, désagréable ; vilain.
until (*prep.*), jusqu'à, *e.g.* jusqu'à 5 heures ; **until then**, jusque-là ; **I shall not leave until seven**, je ne partirai pas avant 7 heures, je ne partirai qu'à 7 heures ; **until** (*conj.*), jusqu'à ce que +*subj.*, *e.g.* je

resterai ici jusqu'à ce que (en attendant que) vous m'appeliez; **to wait until,** attendre que +*subj.*, *e.g.* j'attendrai que vous m'appeliez.

unwell, souffrant.

unwise, imprudent.

up to, jusqu'à; **up till (to) now,** jusqu'ici; **up till (to) then,** jusque-là, jusqu'alors; **he pushed his wheelbarrow up the street,** il poussa sa brouette en montant la rue; **to get up,** se lever, (=*straighten up*) se redresser; **to go (come) up,** monter (*with* être); **to take (bring) up,** monter (*with* avoir); **to bring up** (=*bring near*), approcher, *e.g.* approchez votre chaise; **to go (come) up to,** s'approcher de; **to pick up,** ramasser; **to give up,** livrer, céder, (=*renounce*) renoncer à.

upper, supérieur.

upright (*of persons*), debout.

to upset, bouleverser.

upstairs, en haut.

to urge, engager, *e.g.* je les engage à rentrer chez eux.

to use, employer, se servir de; **to make use of,** se servir de; **what is the use of waiting?** à quoi bon attendre? à quoi sert-il d'attendre? **to get used to,** s'habituer à, s'accoutumer à; **used to,** habitué à, accoutumé à.

useful, utile.

useless, inutile.

usual, habituel; **usually,** d'habitude, d'ordinaire; **as usual,** comme toujours, comme d'habitude, comme d'ordinaire, comme de coutume.

V

vacation, les vacances (*f.*); **long (summer) vacation,** les grandes vacances.

vacuum cleaner, un aspirateur.

vain (=*conceited*), vaniteux; (=*useless*) vain; **in vain,** en vain; **to (do) in vain,** avoir beau (faire), *e.g.* **you may shout in vain, it is no good your shouting,** vous avez beau crier.

valley, la vallée.

value, la valeur.

to vanquish, vaincre (*irr.*).

varied, varié.

vase, le vase.

vast, vaste, immense.

vegetable, le légume.

vehicle, le véhicule, la voiture.

veil, le voile.

velvet, le velours.

vengeance, la vengeance.

veritable, véritable.

very, très, fort, bien.

vestibule, le vestibule.

to vex, vexer, fâcher; **to get vexed,** se vexer, se fâcher; **vexed,** vexé, fâché.

victim, la victime.

victory, la victoire.

view, la vue.

village, le village, (*large*) le bourg; **villager,** le villageois.

vine, la vigne; **vineyard,** la vigne, le vignoble.

vinegar, le vinaigre.

violent, violent; **violently,** violemment; **violence,** la violence.

violin, le violon; **to play the violin,** jouer du violon.

visible, visible.

visit, la visite; **to visit,** visiter, rendre visite à; **to pay a visit to,** rendre visite à; **to go on a**

visit, aller en visite ; **visitor**, le visiteur, *f.* la visiteuse.

vivid (*colour*, *light*, *etc.*), éclatant.

voice, la voix.

voyage, la traversée.

W

to wag (*tail*), remuer.

wagon (*farm*), le chariot.

waistcoat, le gilet.

to wait (for), attendre (vendre), *e.g.* je les attends ; **wait** (*noun*), une attente ; **waiting-room**, la salle d'attente.

waiter, le garçon ; **waitress**, la serveuse.

to waken, éveiller, réveiller ; **to wake up**, s'éveiller, se réveiller ; **to wake up with a start**, s'éveiller en sursaut.

Wales, le Pays de Galles ; **in** (*or* **to**) **Wales**, au Pays de Galles ; **Welsh**, gallois; **Welshman** (**-woman**), le (la) Gallois(e).

walk, la promenade ; **to go for a walk**, faire une promenade ; **walk** (=*gait*), une allure, la démarche ; **walk** (=*path in park, etc.*), une allée.

to walk, marcher ; (*for pleasure*) se promener ; (=*go on foot*) aller à pied, *e.g.* nous y sommes allés à pied ; **to walk up** (*e.g. a street*) monter (*with* avoir) ; **to walk down** (*e.g. a street*), descendre (*with* avoir) ; **to walk away**, s'éloigner ; **to walk toward**, se diriger vers ; **to walk through**, traverser ; **to walk round**, faire le tour de ; **to go at a walking pace**, aller au pas.

walking-stick, la canne.

wall, le mur, la muraille ; **to climb up (over) a wall**, escalader un mur ; **wallpaper**, le papier peint.

wallet, le portefeuille.

walnut, la noix ; **walnut-tree**, le noyer.

to wander, errer.

to want, vouloir (*irr.*), désirer, *e.g.* je veux (désire) acheter des gants.

war, la guerre.

warm, chaud ; **the weather is warm**, il fait chaud ; **I am warm**, j'ai chaud ; **the water is warm**, l'eau est chaude ; **warm** (*of feelings*), chaleureux ; **warmly**, chaleureusement ; **luke-warm**, tiède ; **warmth**, la chaleur.

to warm, chauffer ; **to warm oneself**, se chauffer, se réchauffer.

to warn, avertir (finir) ; **warning**, un avertissement.

to wash, laver ; **to wash oneself**, se laver ; **to wash up** (*crockery, etc.*), faire la vaisselle ; **to wash and get ready**, faire sa toilette, **wash-basin**, le lavabo.

wasp, la guêpe.

to waste, perdre (vendre), gaspiller ; **waste-paper basket**, la corbeille à papier.

watch, la montre ; **wrist-watch**, la montre-bracelet.

to watch, regarder ; **to watch** (*something on the move*), suivre des yeux (du regard) ; **to watch for**, guetter ; **to watch over**, surveiller.

water, l'eau (*f.*) ; **running water**, l'eau courante.

watercress, le cresson.

wave, la vague.

to wave (*the hand, etc.*), agiter.

way (=*road*), le chemin ; **on the way**, en chemin, chemin faisant; **on the way to,** en route pour; **to make one's way towards,** se diriger vers; **to lose one's way,** perdre son chemin, s'égarer; **come this way,** venez par ici; **way out,** la sortie; **a long way (from),** loin (de).

way (=*means*), le moyen.

way (=*fashion, manner*), la façon, la manière; **in this way,** de cette manière (façon); **the way in which,** la manière (façon) dont.

weak, faible; **weakness,** la faiblesse.

wealth, la richesse, les richesses; **wealthy,** riche.

to wear, porter.

weary, las, *f.* lasse; **weariness,** la lassitude.

weather, le temps; **what is the weather like?** quel temps fait-il? **the weather is warm,** il fait chaud; **the weather is cold,** il fait froid; **the weather is fine,** il fait beau (temps); **the weather is bad,** il fait mauvais temps; **weather-beaten,** hâlé; **weather forecast,** les prévisions météorologiques (*abbr.* la météo).

wedding, la noce.

Wednesday, mercredi (*m.*); **next Wednesday,** mercredi prochain.

week, la semaine; huit jours; **next week,** la semaine prochaine; **last week,** la semaine dernière; **today week,** d'aujourd'hui en huit.

to weep, pleurer; **weeping,** pleurant, en pleurs.

to weigh, peser; **weight,** le poids.

welcome, un accueil, la bienvenue; **to welcome,** accueillir (cueillir); **you are welcome,** vous êtes le bienvenu; **to wish anyone welcome,** souhaiter la bienvenue à quelqu'un.

well, bien; **I am well,** je vais bien, je me porte bien; **he is not well,** il ne se porte pas bien, il n'est pas bien portant; **you look well,** vous avez bonne mine; **well!** (*beginning speech*), eh bien! **well and good!** à la bonne heure! **well done!** bravo! **well-behaved,** sage; **as well as,** aussi bien que.

west, l'ouest (*m.*).

to wet, mouiller; **wet,** mouillé, (=*rainy*) pluvieux; **wet to the skin,** mouillé jusqu'aux os.

whale, la baleine.

what; **what are you doing?** que faites-vous? qu'est-ce que vous faites? **I know what is annoying you,** je sais ce qui vous ennuie; **I know what you are doing,** je sais ce que vous faites; **what are you writing with?** avec quoi écrivez-vous? **what book?** quel livre? **what street?** quelle rue? **what!** comment!

whatever I do, quoi que je fasse; **whatever the difficulties may be,** quelles que soient les difficultés.

wheel, la roue; **wheelbarrow,** la brouette.

when, quand; lorsque (*not in questions*); **the day (hour, month, year) when,** le jour (l'heure, le mois, l'année) où; **one day (morning, evening, etc.) when,** un jour (un matin, un soir, etc.) que.

whenever, chaque fois que, toutes les fois que.

where, où ; **where I live there are a lot of vines**, là où j'habite il y a beaucoup de vignes.

whereas, tandis que.

wherever, partout où, *e.g.* partout où je vais.

wherewithal ; **they have not the wherewithal to live**, ils n'ont pas de quoi vivre.

whether, si, *e.g.* je me demande s'il viendra.

while (=*during the time that*), pendant que ; **while, whilst** (*with an idea of contrast*), tandis que.

while (=*period of time*), le moment ; **for a good while**, pendant un bon (long) moment ; **it (that) is not worth while**, ce n'est pas la peine, cela n'en vaut pas la peine.

whip, le fouet ; **to whip**, fouetter.

to **whisper**, chuchoter, murmurer.

whistle, le sifflet ; (=*blast of whistle*) le coup de sifflet ; **to whistle**, siffler.

white, blanc, *f.* blanche ; **white man**, le blanc ; **to whiten**, blanchir (finir) ; **whitewashed**, blanchi à la chaux.

Whitsuntide, la Pentecôte.

whoever, quiconque ; celui qui ; **whoever you are**, qui que vous soyez.

whole, entier, *f.* entière ; **the whole classe**, la classe entière, toute la classe.

wholesome, sain.

whose, dont, *e.g.* un élève dont le travail est bon ; un homme dont je connais le fils ; **whose hat is this?** à qui est ce chapeau?

why, pourquoi.

wicked, méchant, mauvais ; **wickedly**, méchamment ; **wickedness**, la méchanceté.

wide, large ; **this room is 4 metres wide**, cette pièce est large de 4 m ; **he opened his eyes wide**, il ouvrit de grands yeux ; **width**, la largeur.

widow, la veuve ; **widower**, le veuf.

wife, la femme, l'épouse.

wild, sauvage ; (=*unrestrained*) fou, *f.* folle ; (*eyes, look*) hagard ; **wildly**, follement.

will, la volonté ; **where there's a will there's a way**, vouloir c'est pouvoir ; **will you come in?** voulez-vous entrer? **I am quite willing**, je veux bien ; **willingly**, volontiers.

willow, le saule.

to **win**, gagner.

wind, le vent ; **it is windy**, il fait du vent.

to **wind up the clock**, remonter la pendule.

window, la fenêtre ; **to look out of the window**, regarder par la fenêtre ; **window** (*of car or train*), la glace ; **shopwindow**, la vitrine ; **stained-glass window**, le vitrail, *pl.* les vitraux ; **window-pane**, la vitre.

wine, le vin.

wing, une aile ; **to take wing**, s'envoler.

winter, l'hiver (*m.*) ; **in winter**, en hiver ; **a hard winter**, un hiver rigoureux.

to **wipe**, essuyer.

wire, le fil.

wireless, la T.S.F. (la télégraphie sans fil) ; **wireless set**, le poste de T.S.F.

wise, sage.

wish, le désir ; une envie ; **to wish**, vouloir (*irr.*) ; **to wish** (*good morning, good luck, etc.*), souhaiter, *e.g.* je lui souhaitai bonne chance.

wit, l'esprit (*m.*).

with, avec ; **covered** (**filled**, etc.) **with**, couvert (rempli, etc.) de.

without, sans ; **not without hesitation**, non sans hésitation ; **without thinking**, sans penser ; **without his hearing me**, sans qu'il m'entende (*subj.*) ; **to do without**, se passer de, *e.g.* il se passait des plaisirs.

witness, le témoin ; **to witness**, être témoin de.

wolf, le loup.

woman, la femme.

to wonder (=*ask oneself*), se demander.

wonderful, merveilleux ; (*sarcastic*) fameux.

wood, le bois ; **wooden**, de bois ; **wooded**, boisé.

wool, la laine ; **woollen**, de laine.

word, le mot ; la parole ; **upon my word!** ma foi!

work, le travail ; la besogne ; (=*publication*) un ouvrage ; (*literary work, musical, artistic, etc.*) une œuvre ; **he set to work**, il se mit au travail (à l'œuvre) ; **to work**, travailler ; **to work hard**, travailler ferme (dur).

workman, un ouvrier ; **working woman**, une ouvrière.

world, le monde ; **the whole world**, le monde entier.

worm, le ver.

worn out, usé.

worry, l'inquiétude (*f.*), le(s) souci(s) ; **worried**, inquiet, soucieux ; **to worry about, to be worried about**, s'inquiéter au sujet de, se tourmenter au sujet de ; (=*to trouble about*) se soucier de ; **don't worry!** soyez (sois) tranquille!

to worship, adorer.

worth ; **to be worth**, valoir (*irr.*) ; **it** (**that**) **is not worth while**, cela n'en vaut pas **la** peine.

worthy, digne ; brave.

to wound, blesser ; **wound**, la blessure.

to wrap up, envelopper.

wreck, une épave ; **shipwreck**, le naufrage.

to wrest, arracher, *e.g.* il arracha le bâton à l'homme.

wretch, le (la) misérable ; **wretched**, misérable.

wrinkle, la ride ; **wrinkled**, ridé.

wrist, le poignet ; **wrist-watch**, la montre-bracelet.

to write, écrire (*irr.*) ; **writing**, l'écriture (*f.*).

wrong ; **to be wrong**, avoir tort, se tromper ; **I took the wrong road**, je me suis trompé de chemin ; **I went to the wrong house**, je me suis trompé de maison ; **I got out at the wrong place**, je me suis trompé à la descente.

Y

yard, la cour.

year, un an, une année ; **every year**, tous les ans ; **last year**, l'an dernier, l'année dernière ;

next year, l'an prochain, l'année prochaine ; **in the year 1789,** en l'an 1789 ; **for many years,** pendant bien des années ; **the New Year,** le nouvel an ; **New Year's day,** le jour de l'an ; **New Year's gift,** les étrennes (*f.*) ; **a happy New Year!** bonne année!

yellow, jaune.

yesterday, hier ; **yesterday evening,** hier soir.

yet (*adv.*), encore ; **not yet, pas encore.**

yet (*conj.*), pourtant ; **and yet,** et pourtant, et cependant.

to yield, céder.

yonder, là-bas.

young, jeune ; **young lady,** la demoiselle ; **youngster,** le gamin, *f.* la gamine ; **youth,** la jeunesse ; **youth hostel,** l'auberge (*f.*) de la jeunesse.

your (*adj.*), ton (ta *or* tes) ; votre, *pl.* vos ; **yours** (*pron.*), le tien, etc. ; le (la) vôtre, *pl.* les vôtres, *e.g.* ma montre est plus petite que la tienne (la vôtre).

VERB LIST

Infinitive	Participles	Present Indicative	Imperfect Past Hist.	Future Conditional
Avoir, être				
avoir, *to have*	ayant eu	ai, as, a, avons, avez, ont	avais eus	aurai aurais
être, *to be*	étant été	suis, es, est, sommes, êtes, sont	étais fus	serai serais
Donner, Finir, Vendre				
donner, *to give*	donnant donné	donne, -es, -e donnons, -ez, -ent	donnais donnai	donnerai donnerais
finir, *to finish*	finissant fini	finis, -is, -it finissons, -ez,- ent	finissais finis	finirai finirais
vendre, *to sell*	vendant vendu	vends, -s, vend, vendons, -ez, -ent	vendais vendis	vendrai vendrais
Irregular Verbs				
acquérir, *to acquire*	acquérant acquis	acquiers, -s, -t, acquérons, -ez, acquièrent	acquérais acquis	acquerrai acquerrais
aller, *to go*	allant allé	vais, vas, va, allons, allez, vont	allais allai	irai irais
asseoir (Refl. s'asseoir, *to sit down*)	asseyant assis	assieds, -s, assied, asseyons, -ez, -ent	asseyais assis	assiérai assiérais
battre, *to beat*	battant battu	bats, -s, bat, battons, -ez, -ent	battais battis	battrai battrais
boire, *to drink*	buvant bu	bois, -s, boit, buvons, -ez, boivent	buvais bus	boirai boirais
conclure, *to conclude*	concluant conclu	conclus, -s, -t, concluons, -ez, -ent	concluais conclus	conclurai conclurais
conduire, *to lead*	conduisant conduit	conduis, -s, -t, conduisons, -ez, -ent	conduisais conduisis	conduirai conduirais
connaître, *to know*	connaissant connu	connais, -s, connaît, connaissons, -ez, -ent	connaissais connus	connaîtrai connaîtrais

Present Subjunctive	Imperative	Remarks. Verbs similarly conjugated
ie, aies, ait, yons, ayez, aient	aie, ayons, ayez	
ois, sois, soit, oyons, soyez, soient	sois, soyons, soyez	
onne, -es, -e, onnions, -iez, -ent	donne, donnons, donnez	Large group
inisse, -es, -e, inissions, -iez, -ent	finis, finissons, finissez	Large group
ende, -es, -e, endions, -iez, -ent	vends, vendons, vendez	Large group
cquière, -es, -e, cquérions, -iez, cquièrent	acquiers, acquérons, acquérez	conquérir
ille, -es, -e, llions, -iez, aillent	va, allons, allez	Conjugated with être
sseye, -es, -e, sseyions, -iez, -ent	assieds, asseyons, asseyez	Used reflexively : s'asseoir, to sit down
atte, -es, -e, attions, -iez, -ent	bats, battons, battez	combattre, abattre
oive, -es, -e, uvions, -iez, boivent	bois, buvons, buvez	
onclue, -es, -e, oncluions, -iez, -ent	conclus, concluons, concluez	
onduise, -es, -e, onduisions, -iez, -ent	conduis, conduisons, conduisez	produire, construire, réduire, traduire, etc.
onnaisse, -es, -e, onnaissions, -iez, -ent	connais, connaissons, connaissez	paraître, and compounds of both

Infinitive	Participles	Present Indicative	Imperfect Past Hist.	Future Conditional
coudre, *to sew*	cousant cousu	couds, -s, coud, cousons, -ez, -ent	cousais cousis	coudrai coudrais
courir, *to run*	courant couru	cours, -s, -t, courons, -ez, -ent	courais courus	courrai courrais
craindre, *to fear*	craignant craint	crains, -s, -t, craignons, -ez, -ent	craignais craignis	craindrai craindrais
croire, *to believe*	croyant cru	crois, -s, -t croyons, -ez, croient	croyais crus	croirai croirais
croître, *to grow*	croissant crû, *f.* crue	croîs, croîs, croît, croissons, -ez, -ent	croissais crûs	croîtrai croîtrais
cueillir, *to gather*	cueillant cueilli	cueille, -es, -e, cueillons, -ez, ent	cueillais cueillis	cueillerai cueillerais
devoir, *to owe*	devant dû (*f.* due)	dois, -s, -t, devons, -ez, doivent	devais dus	devrai devrais
dire, *to say*	disant dit	dis, -s, -t, disons, dites, disent	disais dis	dirai dirais
dormir, *to sleep*	dormant dormi	dors, -s, -t, dormons, -ez, -ent	dormais dormis	dormirai dormirais
écrire, *to write*	écrivant écrit	écris, -s, -t, écrivons, -ez, -ent	écrivais écrivis	écrirai écrirais
envoyer, *to send*	envoyant envoyé	envoie, -es, -e, envoyons, -ez, envoient	envoyais envoyai	enverrai enverrais
faire, *to do, to make*	faisant fait	fais, -s, -t, faisons, faites, font	faisais fis	ferai ferais
falloir, *to be necessary*	fallu	il faut	il fallait il fallut	il faudra il faudrait
fuir, *to flee*	fuyant fui	fuis, -s, -t, fuyons, -ez, fuient	fuyais fuis	fuirai fuirais
haïr, *to hate*	haïssant haï	hais, -s, -t, haïssons, -ez, -ent	haïssais haïs	haïrai haïrais
lire, *to read*	lisant lu	lis, -s, -t, lisons, -ez, -ent	lisais lus	lirai lirais

Present Subjunctive	Imperative	Remarks. Verbs similarly conjugated
couse, -es, -e, cousions, -iez, -ent	couds, cousons, cousez	
coure, -es, -e, courions, -iez, -ent	cours, courons, courez	accourir, and other compounds
craigne, -es, -e, craignions, -iez, -ent	crains, craignons, craignez	Verbs in -indre, e.g. plaindre, joindre, peindre
croie, -es, -e, croyions, -iez, croient	crois, croyons, croyez	
croisse, -es, -e, croissions, -iez, -ent	croîs, croissons, croissez	accroître
cueille, -es, -e, cueillions, -iez, cueillent	cueille, cueillons, cueillez	accueillir, recueillir
doive, -es, -e, devions, -iez, doivent	dois, devons, devez	
dise, -es, -e, disions, -iez, -ent	dis, disons, dites	
dorme, -es, -e, dormions, -iez, -ent	dors, dormons, dormez	servir, sentir, partir, sortir, mentir, se repentir
écrive, -es, -e, écrivions, -iez, -ent	écris, écrivons, écrivez	décrire, inscrire
envoie, -es, -e, envoyions, -iez, envoient	envoie, envoyons, envoyez	renvoyer
fasse, -es, -e, fassions, -iez, -ent	fais, faisons, faites	
l faille		Used only in 3rd person singular
fuie, -es, -e, fuyions, -iez, fuient	fuis, fuyons, fuyez	s'enfuir
haïsse, -es, -e, haïssions, -iez, -ent	hais, haïssons, haïssez	Begins with *h* aspiré, e.g. je hais
lise, -es, -e, lisions, -iez, -ent	lis, lisons, lisez	relire

Infinitive	Participles	Present Indicative	Imperfect Past Hist.	Future Conditional
mettre, *to put*	mettant mis	mets, -s, met, mettons, -ez, -ent	mettais mis	mettrai mettrais
mourir, *to die*	mourant mort	meurs, -s, -t, mourons, -ez, meurent	mourais mourus	mourrai mourrais
naître, *to be born*	naissant né	nais, -s, naît, naissons, -ez, -ent	naissais naquis	naîtrai naîtrais
nuire, *to harm*	nuisant nui	nuis, -s, -t, nuisons, -ez, -ent	nuisais nuisis	nuirai nuirais
ouvrir, *to open*	ouvrant ouvert	ouvre, -es, -e, ouvrons, -ez, -ent	ouvrais ouvris	ouvrirai ouvrirais
plaire, *to please*	plaisant plu	plais, -s, plaît, plaisons, -ez, -ent	plaisais plus	plairai plairais
pleuvoir, *to rain*	pleuvant plu	il pleut	il pleuvait il plut	il pleuvra il pleuvrait
pouvoir, *to be able*	pouvant pu	peux (puis), -x, -t, pouvons, -ez, peuvent	pouvais pus	pourrai pourrais
prendre, *to take*	prenant pris	prends, -s, prend, prenons, -ez, prennent	prenais pris	prendrai prendrais
recevoir, *to receive*	recevant reçu	reçois, -s, -t, recevons, -ez, reçoivent	recevais reçus	recevrai recevrais
résoudre, *to resolve*	résolvant résolu	résous, -s, -t, résolvons, -ez, -ent	résolvais résolus	résoudrai résoudrais
rire, *to laugh*	riant ri	ris, -s, -t, rions, -ez, -ent	riais ris	rirai rirais
rompre, *to break*	rompant rompu	romps, -s, -t, rompons, -ez, -ent	rompais rompis	romprai romprais
savoir, *to know*	sachant su	sais, -s, -t, savons, -ez, -ent	savais sus	saurai saurais
suffire, *to suffice*	suffisant suffi	suffis, -s, -t suffisons, -ez, -ent	suffisais suffis	suffirai suffirais
suivre, *to follow*	suivant suivi	suis, -s, -t, suivons, -ez, -ent	suivais suivis	suivrai suivrais

Present Subjunctive	Imperative	Remarks. Verbs similarly conjugated
nette, -es, -e, nettions, -iez, -ent	mets, mettons, mettez	permettre, promettre, remettre, omettre
neure, -es, -e, nourions, -iez, meurent	meurs, mourons, mourez	Conjugated with être, e.g. il est mort
aisse, -es, -e, aissions, -iez, -ent	nais, naissons, naissez	renaître
uise, -es, -e, uisions, -iez, -ent	nuis, nuisons, nuisez	
uvre, -es, -e, uvrions, -iez, -ent	ouvre, ouvrons, ouvrez	couvrir, offrir, souffrir
laise, -es, -e, laisions, -iez, -ent	plais, plaisons, plaisez	
pleuve		Used only in 3rd person singular
uisse, -es, -e, uissions, -iez, -ent		
renne, -es, -e, renions, -iez, prennent	prends, prenons, prenez	apprendre, comprendre, surprendre, reprendre
eçoive, -es, -e, ecevions, -iez, reçoivent	reçois, recevons, recevez	apercevoir, décevoir, concevoir
ésolve, -es, -e, ésolvions, -iez, -ent	résous, résolvons, résolvez	
ie, -es, -e, iions, riiez, rient	ris, rions, riez	sourire
ompe, -es, -e, ompions, -iez, -ent	romps, rompons, rompez	interrompre, corrompre
ache, -es, -e, achions, -iez, -ent	sache, sachons, sachez	
uffise, -es, -e, uffisions, -iez, -ent	suffis, suffisons, suffisez	
uive, -es, -e, uivions, -iez, -ent	suis, suivons, suivez	poursuivre

Infinitive	Participles	Present Indicative	Imperfect Past Hist.	Future Conditional
taire (Refl. se taire, *to be* *silent*)	taisant tu	tais, -s, -t, taisons, -ez, -ent	taisais tus	tairai tairais
tenir, *to hold*	tenant tenu	tiens, -s, -t, tenons, -ez, tiennent	tenais tins, -s, -t, tînmes, tîntes, tinrent	tiendrai tiendrais
tressaillir, *to start*	tressaillant tressailli	tressaille, -es, -e, tressaillons, -ez, -ent	tressaillais tressaillis	tressaillirai tressaillirai
vaincre, *to vanquish*	vainquant vaincu	vaincs, -s, vainc, vainquons, -ez, -ent	vainquais vainquis	vaincrai vaincrais
valoir, *to be worth*	valant valu	vaux, -x, -t, valons, -ez, -ent	valais valus	vaudrai vaudrais
venir, *to come*	venant venu	viens, -s, -t, venons, -ez, viennent	venais vins, -s, -t, vînmes, vîntes, vinrent	viendrai viendrais
vivre, *to live*	vivant vécu	vis, -s, -t, vivons, -ez, -ent	vivais vécus	vivrai vivrais
voir, *to see*	voyant vu	vois, -s, -t, voyons, -ez, voient	voyais vis	verrai verrais
vouloir, *to wish*	voulant voulu	veux, -x, -t, voulons, -ez, veulent	voulais voulus	voudrai voudrais

Present Subjunctive	Imperative	Remarks. Verbs similarly conjugated
aise, -es, -e, aisions, -iez, -ent	tais, taisons, taisez	Used reflexively : se taire, to be (become) silent
ienne, -es, -e, enions, -iez, tiennent	tiens, tenons, tenez	contenir, retenir, appartenir, maintenir, etc.
ressaille, -es, -e, ressaillions, -iez, -ent	tressaille, tressaillons, tressaillez	
ainque, -es, -e, ainquions, -iez, -ent	vaincs, vainquons, vainquez	convaincre
aille, -es, -e, alions, -iez, vaillent	vaux, valons valez	
ienne, -es, -e, enions, -iez, viennent	viens, venons, venez	devenir, revenir, convenir, parvenir
ive, -es, -e, ivions, -iez, -ent	vis, vivons, vivez	survivre, revivre
oie, -es, -e, oyions, -iez, voient	vois, voyons, voyez	revoir
euille, -es, -e, oulions, -iez, veuillent	veuille, veuillons, veuillez	

l'oiseau
le toit
la lucarne
les feuilles
le nid
la fenêtre
le drapeau
la mère du maire
1882
MAIRIE
la porte
les volets
RESTAURANT
l'arbre (m)
la chemise
le garçon
l'échelle
le maire
l'homme
le boucher
le cheval
le petit garçon
le boulanger
le facteur
la sacoche
le jeu de boules
la bicyclette
le canard
le canard